Haunting the Past:

History, Memory, Dreams and the Reflections of a Dying Historian

By

Joseph Laythe

Dedicated to:

Fr. Gene Peoples and Sr. Mary Claire Kennedy

Table of Contents

Acknowledgments

My most important debt of gratitude goes to whatever Great Maker there is and for the blessed life I have loved to live. I am eternally part of that cosmic chemical mix. I recognize that I have not done it alone. I have been nurtured, taught, mentored, carried, and buoyed over the course of 50 years by hundreds and hundreds of great people. I am thankful for all the assistance those individuals gave me, whether they knew it or not. For every individual listed below there are countless folks who have done similar acts of kindness on my behalf, many of whom were simply passers-by or one-time acquaintances; from the nuns on the bullet train in Japan to the two old ladies who gave me a ride in Canada, they have all contributed in some measure to my success.

But there are those who absolutely need to know how grateful I am for their friendship, love, and aid. I thank my wife, Chris, for bearing my burdens and loving me for the last quarter century. My daughters, Lydia and Isabella, have loved me, inspired me and, like their mother, made me a better man. I can only hope that whatever memories they will keep of me will be ones that make them smile or make them proud.

I am grateful for the help and love and support from my family and friends all across this country: Jeri and Ken Chaitin, Tom Laythe, Nadine Ford, Steve and Nellie Malany, J. Michael and Theresa Keyes, Clay Conner, Walt Bithell, Brian and Ruthie Keyes, Dominic and Alexei Cifrese, Mary Keyes, Rick and Ka Bruya, Kathy and Randy Gillam, Jo Ellen and Roger Crisafi, Christine and John Hodges, Bernice Pope, Susan Keyes, Mike and Sandy Callahan, Wade and Michelle Callahan, Carol Trusty Bonney, Mandy and Bryce Fauble, Tracy Leet, Alicia Twilla, Race and Kevin Lynch, Chuck and Stacy Burt, Meg and Alex Durkin.

I was strengthened daily from a wide range of friends like Patty and Bruce Bechhold, Jim McColly, Scott Hexum, Todd Polly (and his salmon), Brian Canady, Fr. Greg Smith, Sharon French, Betty McInturff, Pat Dixson, Daren Fluke, Brett Walker, Sharlet Driggs, Fr. Greg Smith, Chris Racicot, Carol Wilson Bergstrom, Karen Barnhardt, Geoff Gallus, Sam Artzis, and Melvin Nair; And, to a special band of social justice crusaders (many of whom I grew up with in Idaho in the face of staunch white privilege): Kim Eddins, Monica Gabica Trivette, Lincoln Newell, Scott Marker, Mack McCoy, Scott Kane, Suzy Arnold Venezia, Rick Boger-Hawkins, Machelle Migneault, Paul Beddoe, Martha Wharry Turner, Cathy Kearns, Nick Musser, Mali Sarriugarte Lajciak, and Michael Donovan.

I must also give special thanks to Edinboro University for allowing me to do what I love: study history and teach. Special thanks to my friends and colleagues: Jerra Jenrette, Trish Hillman, Theresa Thewes, Naod Kebede, Bob Hass, Cynthia Legin-Bucell, Terri Astorino, Melissa Gibson-Hancox, Tom White, Corinne Schaeffer, Hank Lawrence, Jody Gallagher, Ihor Bemko, Jim Fischer, Elvage Murphy, Melissa Burnett, Peg Shorts, Sue Wilkosz, Mary Jo Melvin, Janet Bowker, Corbin Fowler, Robert Weber, Peg and Dick Bevevino, Sherry Reynolds, Sezai Demiral, Jim Wertz, and Ron Spiller. I am especially grateful for the help of Frank Pogue, James Moran, Julie Wollman, Judy Kubeja, and Mike Hannan.

I could not have lasted as long as I did without the incredible care provided by the Cleveland Clinic, its staff, physicians, and other caregivers. Special thanks goes to Dr. G. Thomas Budd, Dr. Steven Lietman, Dr. Daniel Raymond, Dr. Maggie Saverino Glenn, Dr. Dustin Thompson, and Dr. S. Sethi, Armandi Moeharam, Maricar Gomez, Roberta Davis, Arthur Merritt, and Bryan Kinney.

I was also buoyed in spirit by my friends and mentors within the Sisters of St. Joseph, most notably: Sr. Mary Claire Kennedy, Sr. Claire Marie Beichner, Sr. Stephanie and Sr. Andre. They furthered my faith and my desire to serve that had been born out of my experiences at Carroll College with Fr. William Greytak, Fr. Jeremiah Sullivan, and Fr. Gene Peoples.

In addition, it is only appropriate to recognize my academic mentors and role models: Dr. Louise Wade, Dr. Richard Maxwell Brown, Dr. David Johnson, Dr. Gordon Dodds, Dr. Bernard Burke, Dr. Matthew Dennis, Dr. Robert Swartout, Dr. Robert Archibald, and Dr. Glenn May. I apologize for those times when I did not uphold the highest standards of our discipline—when my footnotes got sloppy or when my writing did not get the editing attention it deserved. This work itself did not go through the traditional peer review process and I am disheartened by that fact. But, I am afraid that otherwise it would have simply been thrown away.

Lastly, I was always inspired and energized by my students. It is with special fondness that I thank Nathan Aulenbacher, Stacy Cornwell Christe, Tom Scarpone, Justin Crousey, Tanya Teglo, Jill Constantin, Michael Haider, Amy Punsky and Laura McNeill, Erin Sullivan, Michael Kleber, Meredith Supinski, Andrew Miller, Gary Cirelli, Rob Thornton, Greg Anysz, John Lyons, Selma Sinanovic, Sharon Yost, Anthony Sufra, Allison and Steve Martin, Josh Blood, Josh Schaldenbrand, Luis Rodriguez, Mark Deka, Brandon Fahey, Rachel Mansfield, Marc Sanko, Marvin DeBose, Eric Rees, Tom Giles, Andrew Miller, Steve Romanchak, Lydia Devault-Arn, Andreanna Mond, Jasmine Jones, Eugene Turner, Nadia Boussalham, Sam Bertolino, Dave Markley, Mejkan Tague, Nate Beamer, Stacey Turner, Jamie Chapman, and Jaime Price Anderson. There are hundreds and hundreds of other students who changed me and made me a better person. We never do it alone.

We all make epic journeys; it's called life. I had a remarkable trip and I am grateful that perhaps in some way I have made the planet a better place for having existed. I am hopeful that I have had a lasting impact on those with whom I had contact.

Foreword

On March 22, 2013, my wife and I were enjoying a Friday night cocktail at home. As I sipped my cherry-flavored Evan Williams and listened to the events of her workday, I was subtly aware of the growing tenderness in my left thigh. Then, the phone rang. It was Dr. Jeffrey Clemente, our family physician. As I snuck away to the living room to hear better, he proceeded to tell me that the biopsy results had come back and that I was now diagnosed with myxofibrosarcoma, a malignant cancer of the connective tissue between my muscle and the femur of my left leg. My suspicions about that tenderness had come true. I had only noticed the lump in my leg a month before and when it started there was absolutely no pain whatsoever. When it did get tender a few weeks later, I visited Dr. Clemente and was subsequently subjected to a series of x-ray examinations, sonograms, venous evaluations, and ultimately the biopsy. Almost immediately, I sought the medical

expertise of orthopedic oncologists at the Cleveland Clinic some

100 or so miles to the west of the small college town in which I

lived. Over the following two and one-half years, I was

subjected to more tests, a second and a third more painful

biopsy, pre-operative tests, the removal of my femur, surgical

installation of a prosthetic femur, and radiation. During that

time, it was discovered that it had metastasized to my lungs and

so I had two major lung surgeries, a kidney surgery, a brutal

chemotherapy treatment for six months, and yet the little

tumors aren't yet dead and gone and out of my lower torso

body.

    It was, in the course of this life-changing development,

that I began to reflect upon my life and all that had transpired

since my birth in 1965, marriage in 1989, and my hiring as a

history professor in 1996. It was not that I only questioned

what had happened (the proverbial "why me?" scenario), but to

also question my work as a historian and its value. This, in itself,

was nearly heresy. It was, for me, an act of sacrilege to

question what had defined me and what had shaped my overall worldview. History and the act of seeing the world through a historical lens (historicism) was everything to me. Every semester for the last 20 years, I rose before my students and talked about what history was (and was not) and then shared with them what I found to be the most compelling and gratifying and rewarding element of the college experience: that each discipline sought to understand and answer the fundamental human question "who are we?" and "how do we fit in?"

I discussed with those students how each university discipline (most, but not all) answer those questions within the framework of that discipline. Biologists might explain who we are by showing what we are and how that biological arrangement shapes who we are and what we do. Chemists might answer the question from a fundamental element position; that we are simply a series of chemical formations resting in and mingling in a large cosmic chemical pool. Psychologists might define who we are by our brains; artists might argue that who we are is defined by our unique ability to create art; sociologists might say it's defined by how we relate to one another, and so on. Historians argue that the best way to understand who we are as a people (whether that be as a species, nation, or community) is by understanding where we came from and how we got to where we are today. In short, historians believe the best way to know "who we are" is to see who we were. I believed that and had shared those convictions (often very convincingly) with my students for years on end. I may still believe that, but I am prepared here to introduce some ideas that may, in fact, change it or modify it such that we may need to re-think our notions of "history" and its value as well as re-think "who are we?" After all, maybe James Baldwin was right when he wrote, "People are trapped in history, and history is trapped in them."[1] I increasingly understood that history as the record of human experience might be horribly flawed. Human experience as a template for learning was, after all,

---

[1] Peter Archer, *The Quotable Intellectual.* Avon, MA: Adams Media, 2010, 106.

replete with obvious and blatant errors, contradictions,

hypocrisy, and folly. History was no better as a discipline than

the subjects it studied.

This work, therefore, is an effort to lay out for the

reader the process of that change and modification that went

through my head and heart in the spring of 2013. To get us

through this transformation, however, it will be necessary to

cover some old ground. In the early sections of this work, I will

highlight the traditional definitions of history and its value. I will

at the end of those sections, however, begin to question why

we choose certain elements to include, the small role bias plays,

and the more important notion of a "collective memory." In the

second part of this work I will wrestle with "memory." I will

examine the science behind memory, the value of memory, and

how memories are naturally distorted over time. This

examination of memory and its processes within the human

brain will then lead me into the third part of this work: dreams.

I will examine in this section the known science of dreaming,

historical theories of dreaming, and its value. I will then use the last section to weave together some ideas about dreaming and the human brain, memory, and our collective past. Throughout it all, I will be using personal anecdotes and my reflections on my own human experience, my own troubled past, and my impending death to not only weave the story into a more fluid narrative, but to inform the reader that this a fundamental human experience. I am not the first, nor the last to go through it. This is a statement of blatant obviousness. We all die and we all remember (in various ways and in varying degrees) our own past. Where, in this process, do history, memory, and dreams collide? Is it here, on the footsteps of my own grave? And will it serve us any good to think about it in advance of these cataclysmic turning points? I will, as you might already suspect, argue that we can all benefit from such self-reflection. As one prominent historian has noted, "Whatever the figure of speech through which it is expressed, thought issues from the common ground of humankind's imaginative efforts to make sense of its lived experience. The historian discovers the constancy of this human capacity for creativity in the face of

changing realities."[2]

---

[2] Patrick H. Hutton, *History as an Art of Memory* Hanover, NH: University Press of New England, 1993, 48.

CHAPTER ONE

History: Our Collective Memory?

Introduction

Everyone has studied history in one way or another. From Mrs. McGillicuddy's 3rd grade class to Mr. Potratz's 11th grade world civilizations class, it is and has been a hallmark in American education. Our notion of history, what it constitutes and what its value is has, however, changed over the course of time. History, for all intents and purposes, has been subject to historical [illegible] to many, a subject [illegible] they loved in school. [illegible] yet, [illegible] relationship was largely born out of a poor educational system. Coach Schmucker's pathetic, but indifferent presentation on the past bored students. He failed to make a connection between the students and that past and, perhaps more importantly, he failed to make a connection between himself and the material. Students, as a result, failed to see the relevancy, the potency, and immediacy of the past. But history is and has been so much more than simply the names and dates Coach Schmucker asked us to memorize. Today, history can be said to be three distinct things: the past, the interpretations of the past, and the professional discipline that examines both the past and the various interpretations.

The Past

History is, in its most simple form, everything that happened before now. The fact that just moments ago you read the previous sentence is history. It is in the past. It occurred in a time that cannot be re-captured or re-created. It is a unchanging "it happened." Any human event before now—wars, elections, assassinations, births and deaths, migrations and so on all constitute history because they occurred in the past. But history is not simply reserved for the wars and elections, movement of troops, and dry lists of facts. History, by virtue of this first definition, constitutes all human behavior—the lovemaking, the crimes, the thefts, the mundane acts of humans at an everyday level and on an everyday basis.

They are in the past and, as a result, part of history. In my college classroom, I might ask my students a series of odd questions. I might ask, "How many of you, in the brief period you have been on the campus this week, have had a bowel movement?" They invariably chuckle and shyly raise their hands. As an aside, as a professional I also believe it behooves me to make another statement on the heels of the previous question: "If you did not raise your hand, I would suggest you seek medical attention. It's a human function, get help." But, I then turn the issue back to its original point: those actions of my students constituted history. Their bowel movements occurred, they are in the past, they are concrete and unchanging. You cannot take them back nor would you want to. Sadly, there probably is some weird graduate student at Yale studying the bowel movements of New York City Irishmen between 1854 and 1855 as part of their doctoral dissertation. But, it cannot be denied. If it was before now, it was history and is history.

Of course, here in a moment, we'll refine this a bit when we talk about "interpretations" of the past, but we can see that history is a pretty big topic. It is a topic that covers 7 continents, thousands of years, and billions of people. It is concrete and unchanging, but it is also immense and growing exponentially. At this point, we are not worried about how we can *know* that past and with what kind of accuracy and authority we can make claims about that concrete past. What we can say is that it did and it *was*. Moreover, and again I will border on blasphemy within my own professional discipline when I ask the question, to what degree has our commitment to "objectivity" obscured the role of history? Reza Aslan notes, "The notion of history as a critical analysis of observable and verifiable events in the past is a product of the modern age...." Others in the past, he further notes, "for whom history was not a matter of uncovering *facts*, but of revealing *truths*." In short, has the mission of history obscured the function?

The Interpretation of the Past

History grows as a subject every moment we are alive. Today's textbooks on U.S. History include brief sections on the

Bush regime and the Obama administration. This, of course,

was not in the textbooks I had as a college student because they

had not happened yet. So, the history we know and the history

we can study expands with time. In some cases, for the sake of

physical space in a textbook or because of limited time in the

classroom, we have to condense these histories down. We

know what happened in 1921, but perhaps because of those

limitations we cannot give it the same space or time or level of

consideration that we give to 1973.[3] This is, for a historian, one

of the sad facts of our trade. World History, at least in the

classroom, gets as much time and as many pages of text as does

U.S. History. Whereas the history of the presidential

administration of Rutherford B. Hayes (a four year span

between 1877 and 1880) might get 2 pages, the administration

of John F. Kennedy (which last less than three years) gets

significantly more. It takes up more time in our lectures and

space in our texts because it is more recent, more

---

[3] Eviatar Zerubavel, *Time Maps: Collective Memory and the Social Shape of the Past.* Chicago: University of Chicago Press, 2003, 27-29.

contemporary, and seemingly more relevant. I would, of course, challenge that last supposition. Yet, both the Hayes and Kennedy Administration (a total of seven years) gets more coverage in the texts and course lectures than some decades, centuries, and millennia in our ancient past. This is "historical focusing." The question becomes: Have we condensed our stories and reduced the facts about the past to gross generalizations because we have to in order to tell the story? If this is acceptable, then what is wrong with filmmakers reducing their scripts and storylines on historical subjects to fit the parameters of the film? Have we forgotten that history is a lesson and that those lessons about our past can be told in a variety of ways and that ownership of that past is not exclusively held by professional historians, but all members of the public?

Those considerations of "time" and "space" force humans to make judgments about the Past. As historians, we ferret through all the primary and secondary literature and assess, based on our professional experience and filtered through our personal experiences, which events of the human past are worth addressing within the expressed time and space given to us. This means historians (and all humans who think about the past) make interpretations of the past. For some, this will seem like bias is guiding our understanding of the past. I am not one who likes the word "bias," however. It smacks of deliberate negligence or an act of malicious intent. Instead, I'd suggest that we can safely use the term "social values" shape our interpretations of the past. There are a variety of social values within any given society and they subconsciously govern our behaviors. This means that there are a variety of different interpretations of that "past." Some southern historian might interpret the Civil War as an act of "Northern aggression" while a northern historian might regard the Confederacy as an act of war by traitorous and treacherous slave owners. In the end, value is gained by having multiple interpretations as they begin to more accurately grasp the "real" feelings and sentiments of that "past." Because historians write a narrative of the past that encompasses thousands if not millions of people, it not only reasons that the more historians write about the past, the more perspectives are gained about that past, but a greater portion of that past's true character is being represented in the literature.

So, within any given time period, there may be a variety of historians writing different interpretations of the past. Differences in interpretation arise, in part, because of different sets of data and new evidence introduced into the literature. Historian A believes one thing about an event because he's examined one-half of the existing record. Historian B believes something altogether different because she has examined the other half of the existing record. Historian C jumps in, synthesizes the two interpretations after having examined the entire body of evidence, and espouses a new hybrid interpretation. Lastly, Historian D comes out with a landmark work with an altogether new interpretation because some scrolls were discovered in some obscure cave and have been linked to the time and place being examined. Historians can only assess the past with the limited evidence available to them:

written records, archaeological evidence, scientific data, photographs and the like. As we progress through time, we have inevitably found more evidence about the past, exposed new strands that tell us more about that period under study, and expand the characters of value in the study. In class, I always use the case of the historian George Kahin who in the late 1960s wrote one of the first scathing histories of President Lyndon Johnson and his policies on Vietnam. By the 1990s, because of the Freedom of Information Act and his access to Johnson's White House tapes, Kahin was forced to revise his interpretation of LBJ from a froth-at-the-mouth anti-communist warhawk to a moderate who consistently (in the face of his own inherited Harvard Boys advisors) called for greater restraint in Vietnam. I have great respect for Kahin for few historians (like most academics) are willing to admit they were initially wrong. But, Kahin demonstrated that new evidence altered his perspective of LBJ.[4] In short, new evidence changes interpretations.

---

[4] George M. Kahin, *Intervention: How America became Involved in*

More importantly, however, it is worth noting that those interpretations change over the course of time. In the 1890s, for example, very few historians wrote about the historical experiences of African-Americans, women, or criminals. Why? Because in the 19th century, social values suggested that those individuals experiences mattered less to "history" and their roles in determining the fate of nations was small. Of course, today we know better. We know that the United States was built upon the backs of African-Americans through that insidious institution known as slavery; that women were central to this nation's economy and government and, if for no other reason, constituted roughly 50% of the population; and that criminals, while perhaps the underbelly of American society, were instrumental (through their acts) in the formation of American laws and institutions. Moreover, one might also be able to assess American power and the relative "greatness" and "exceptionalness" of the United States more

---

Vietnam. New York: Knopf, 1986 and George Kahin and John Lewis, *The United States in Vietnam*. New York: Delta, 1967.

through how we dealt with Blacks, women, and criminals than the "Great White Men" who governed us at the time. Social values changed. Over the course of the twentieth century, Americans (in part because of their changing views of the past) came to regard those three social sub-groups as more important, as subjects worthy of greater study. So, in the 1960s and 1970s, we began to see a flourishing of African-American studies. In the 1970s and 1980s, we saw women's history emerge as a powerful and important sub-field. In the 1990s, we began to see examinations of crime and criminals expand. Because social values changed, historical interpretations changed. So, while the past (History in is most simple form) is concrete and unchanging, interpretations of that past are numerous, changing, and dynamic.[5]

---

[5] See Arnesen, Eric. "Up From Exclusion: Black and White Workers, Race, and the State of Labor History," *Reviews in American History* 26(1) March 1998: 146–174; Dagbovie, Pero Gaglo. "Exploring a Century of Historical Scholarship on Booker T. Washington." *Journal of African American History* 2007 92(2): 239–264; Dorsey, Allison. "Black History Is American History: Teaching African American History in the Twenty-first Century.*" Journal of American History* 2007 93(4): 1171–1177; Ernest, John. "Liberation Historiography: African-American Historians before the Civil War," *American Literary History* 14(3), Fall 2002: 413–443; Franklin, John Hope. "Afro-American History: State of

My students will sometimes ask why that idea about "changing interpretations" is important to know. I tell them two things. First, whenever you read anything, you need to consider the source and subject. This is particularly important today in our world of information illiteracy. We are bombarded with articles, news footage, and websites that purport to be objective, factual, and informative. We often fail to recognize that they have explicit business objectives and/or political agendas and that they often (more than we 'd like to admit) distort the evidence to fit their larger goals. Knowing the source, authorship, objectives and agenda allow us to assess the reliability of the works and place it in the appropriate context. Thus, it allows us to read a 1915 work on slavery and the American South and understand what it's about and what it means. It allows us to turn what was a secondary source on

the Art," *Journal of American History* (June 1988): 163–173; Harris, Robert L., "Coming of Age: The Transformation of Afro-American Historiography," *Journal of Negro History* 57 (1982): 107–121; Higginbotham, Evelyn Brooks, "African-American Women's History and the Metalanguage of Race," *Signs: Journal of Women in Culture and Society* 17 (1992): 251–274; Meier, August, and Elliott Rudwick. *Black History and the Historical Profession, 1915–1980.* Champaign-Urbana: University of Illinois Press, 1986.

slavery (written after the abolition of that institution) into a primary source about early 20th century interpretations of slavery (written at that time in the early 20th century).

So, historians not only study the "past" and make "interpretations of the past" but we also study the history of the study of history. This is called "historiography." Historiography is the study of how history has changed over the course of time. Again, my students will ask "why is this important?" I will, of course, quickly retort "Isn't critical thinking enough?" They stare at me blankly and so I argue on. I ask them, "How many of you own a car or at least drive one?" And most of them raise their hands. I then ask "How many of you own a car or drive a car even though you know it pollutes the environment?" Most hands remain raised, although some begrudgingly. Then I ask, "How many of you own a car or drive a car, even though you know it pollutes the environment AND that that pollution is going to come at the cost of your grandkids and great grandkids and that someday, your thoughtlessness, selfishness, and laziness may mean your great-great grandchildren will have to wear plastic helmets over their heads and look out at the toxic world they live in with three distorted eyes from the sides of their warped little heads?" Of course, they laugh, but they get it. I remind them that the historians of the future are not going to say "Oh, they just didn't know any better." No, historians won't say that because historians will know that we knew better and despite that knowledge we continued to ruin our planet. We will all someday be subject to historical scrutiny and historical judgment. There might be some folks, like those historians today who rationalize southern plantation owners' treatment of slaves, who will absolve you of your sins, our sins. But, maybe, the value of understanding the value of "changing interpretations" is not only to know that we are experiencing them, but our actions today will be forever judged by them. As Edward Gibbon once wrote, "I have but one lamp by which my feet are guided, and that is the lamp of experience.[6] I know no way of judging the future but by the

---

[6] Patricia B. Craddock, *Edward Gibbon, Luminous Historian 1772–1794*. Baltimore: Johns Hopkins University Press, 1989.

past."[7] Or as Patrick Hutton has adeptly (and ironically) noted, "In recollection, we do not retrieve images of the past as they were originally perceived but rather as they fit into our present conceptions."[8]

Historiography (or a Brief History of History) and Schools of Interpretation

Now, having identified that history is not just the past (all that occurred before), but a thoughtful interpretation of that past based on contemporary social values and the personal experiences of the historian, it is worth noting here (as briefly as I can) the different schools of historical thought. The value in examining this quick historiographical lesson is not to dull your wits and hypnotize your brain with the tedium of different historians' train of thought, but to illustrate how history has "changed" and how (as we'll see later) these "changes" might

---

[7] Archer, 103.
[8] Hutton, 7.

reflect the "plasticity" of the past much like the plasticity of memory and the plasticity of the brain. This is not, by any means, intended to be an exhaustive examination of the schools of thought, but rather a simplified condensed version and interpretation of these basic schools.

Pre-Historic Historians

Most of my professional colleagues will probably disagree with me here, but I believe that prehistoric humans, the paleo-peoples of long ago, and others beyond the pale of what we call the ancient civilized world also created history. If they remembered their past and attempted to re-tell that past in one way or another (written or not), then they were historians. Their stories and their tales of their past have been called by us as "creation myths." We have called them that in the past as they were clearly infused with legend, fantastical stories of monsters and strange creatures, and lacked evidence or scientific merit. Yet, this is a disservice to our ancient ancestors. Their stories did as much for them as Our "histories" do for us---they preserved the group's identity, offered

guidance to them in their dangerous, hostile world and

established values by which the group ought to operate.[9]

So, these folks whom we often regard as knuckle-

dragging savages lived by the same mental processes we do

today. They work and live, remember, and then work and live

for more based on those memories. The collective memories

became their histories. They were not told in dusty old books

and dry college lectures, but through incredible storytelling

around the fire. Imagine, after a long day of hunting and

gathering somewhere in central Europe or in the woodlands of

northeastern North America, the people gather around a fire for

protection and heat. Their food would have been roasting over

spits. Imagine children running and skipping around the

periphery with their cousins, being chided by that one grumpy

aunt, and then the elder steps forward to tell a story. It is a

---

[9] See Alice Beck Kehoe, *Shamans and Religion: An Anthropological Exploration in Critical Thinking*. New York: Waveland Inc., 2000; Ian G. Barbour, Ian G. *Religion and Science: Historical and Contemporary Issues*. San Francisco: Harper, 1997; and Dawn E. Bastian and Judy K. Mitchell. *Handbook of Native American Mythology*. Santa Barbara: ABC-CLIO, 2004.

story of their past, how they came to where they are and how they came to be. His story might be infused with magical creatures or earthly specimens with special powers. There is a greater communion between the animals and the people and his story reflects that. His story is not filled with data, names and dates, stats, maps, but poetic descriptions of "the people." This shaman is an elder, a leader, a poet and a historian. His words remind the people of who they are, not just in name and deed, but in values and principles. He reminds them of their connection to one another and to the world. His stories explain "turning points" in their story---how they came to move from the mountains onto the plains, about the catastrophic flood that swept down the river gorge and killed so many children, of the "others" who attacked them. It is not a conventional history as we would define it today, but it was a "keeping of the past"; it was a group's memory. The shaman was a poet historian. For example, a story from the Wasco people of the Columbia River region in Oregon.

"The Elk, the Hunter, and His Greedy Father" Wasco

There was a man at Dog River [Hood River] in days gone
by, whose wife was with child. Pretty soon she gave
birth to a boy. While she was sick, the man carried
wood, and one day a piece of bark fell on his forehead
and cut him. When the boy was large enough to shoot,
he killed birds and squirrels, he was a good shot. One
day, however, his father said to him, "You don't do as I
used to. I am ashamed to own you. When I was your
age, I used to catch young elks. One day when I killed a
young elk, the old one attacked me and made me this
scar you see on my forehead."

Then the boy had a visit from an elk, and the elk said, "If
you will serve me and hear what I say, I will be your
master and will help you in every necessity. You must
not be proud. You must not kill too many of any animal.
I will be your guardian spirit."

So the young man became a great hunter, knew where
every animal was—elk, bear, deer. He killed what he
needed for himself, and no more. The old man, his
father, said to him, "You are not doing enough. At your
age I used to do much more." The young man was
grieved at his father's scolding. The elk, the young
man's helper, was very angry at the old man. At last
[he] helped the young man to kill five whole herds of
elk. He killed all except his own spirit elk, though he
tried without knowing it to ill even [that one]. This elk
went to a lake and pretended to be dead; the young
man went into the water to draw the elk out, but as
soon as he touched it, both sank.

After touching bottom, the young man woke as from a
sleep, and saw bears, deer, and elks without number,
and they were all persons. Those that he had killed
were there too, and they groaned. A voice called,
"Draw him in." Each time the voice was heard, he was
drawn nearer his master, the Elk, until he was at his
side. Then the great Elk said, "Why did you go beyond

what I commanded? Your father required more of you than he himself ever did. Do you see our people on both sides? These are they whom you have killed. You have inflicted many needless wounds on our people. Your father lied to you. He never saw my father, as he falsely told you, saying that my father had met him. He also told you that my father gave him a scar. That is not true; he was carrying fire-wood when you were born, and a piece of bark fell on him and cut him. He has misled you. Now I shall leave you, and never be your guardian spirit again."

When the Elk had finished, a voice was heard saying five times, "Cast him out." The young man went home. The old man was talking, feeling well. The young man told his two wives to fix a bed for him. They did so. He lay there five days and nights, and then told his wives, "Heat water to wash me, also call my friends so that I may talk to them. Bring five elk-skins." All this was done. The people came together, and he told them, "My father was dissatisfied because, as he said, I did not do as he had done. What my father wanted grieved the guardian spirit which visited and aided me. My father deceived me. He said that he had been scarred on the head by a great elk while taking the young elk away. He said that I was a disgrace to him. He wanted me to kill more than was needed. He lied. The spirit has left me, and I die."[10]

This story was likely born out of a previous experience among the Wasco people where they had depleted their resources. Re-told by a leader it served as a reminder to those

[10] Jarold Ramsey, comp and ed., *Coyote Was Going There: Indian Literature of the Oregon Country* (Seattle: University of Washington Press, 1977): 64-65.

future generations of the challenges brought by not being in greater harmony with nature and not heeding the advice of their internal spirit guardians. It was an effective use of the "past" in the "present" to guide the Wascos through the "future." It was an imaginative effort to understand the past and their shared experiences and apply those lessons to their current lives. It was a historical lesson.

Ancient Historians

Then, as we enter the "civilized" eras and we begin to see permanent settlements, agriculture, urbanization, and specialized labor, we also begin to see the development of writing. The development of writing, in almost every culture, shifted the power of storytelling and history-making to an elite sub-group of society. Only those with special skills could write "the past" and only a select few had the skills to read that "past." Now, storytelling and poetry don't go away, they just shift toward theatre and oratory. They'll remain vibrant elements in every society, but the "Past" has now been reserved for those who have the means and the power. It was, perhaps, abundantly clear to those who held the power that the individual who shapes the history of a people also shapes the vision and values of the people and, in doing so, shapes the future of that same people. Whereas the "past" had been relatively egalitarian, shared around the fire, and heard by the old and young, powerful and not-so-powerful, history under the ancients was now an elite preserve to a certain degree.

The stories they told were mixtures of omens and magic as well as descriptions of wars and emperors, high-level cabals and royal intrigue. They rarely addressed the actions, activities and needs of the lower people. They may have mused about values in certain tracts, but they increasingly became focused on those actions at the highest levels.

Thucydides (460-400BCE) and Herodotus (484-425BCE) stand out as the greatest of ancient historians.[11] Herodotus, the

---

[11] Sharlene Sayegh and Eric Altice, *History and Theory*. New York: Pearson Education, Inc., 2014, 8.

"father of history" and author of *The Histories*, wrestled with

the reliability of sources, conducted personal research (which

involved travel) and emphasized the character of men. He also,

of course, in keeping with the times, also noted the role of the

Divine in the shaping of the course of human experience, but

kept it at a safe distance.

Thucydides eliminated the role of the Divine as much as

he could and emphasized rational arguments. His reasoned

assessment of the Pelopponesian War was an advancement in

critical analysis.[12]

---

[12] Sayegh and Altice, 9. See also Charles Norris Cochrane, *Thucydides and the Science of History*, New York: Oxford University Press, 1929; W. Robert Connor, *Thucydides*. Princeton: Princeton University Press 1984; Carolyn Dewald, *Thucydides' War Narrative: A Structural Study.* Berkeley, CA: University of California Press, 2006; John Huston Finley, , *Thucydides*, Cambridge, Massachusetts : Harvard University Press, 1947; Steven Forde, *The Ambition to Rule : Alcibiades and the Politics of Imperialism in Thucydides*. Ithaca : Cornell University Press, 1989; T.J. Luce, *The Greek Historians*. London: Routledge,1997; Arnaldo Momigliano, *The Classical Foundations of Modern Historiography.* Sather Classical Lectures, 54 , Berkeley: University of California Press 1990; and Perez Zagorin, *Thucydides: an Introduction for the Common Reader*. Princeton, NJ: Princeton University Press, 2005. For Herodotus, see: Aubrey De Selincourt, *The World of Herodotus*. London: Secker and Warburg, 1962; J. A. S. Evans, *The Beginnings of History: Herodotus and the Persian Wars*. Campbellville, Ont.: Edgar Kent, 2006; J.A.S. Evans, *Herodotus*. Boston: Twayne, 1982; John Gould, *Herodotus*. New York: St. Martin's Press, 1989; Francois Hartog, "The Invention of History: The Pre-History of a Concept from Homer to

Medieval Historians

During the Middle Ages, historians were largely centered on Christian historical developments. This is not surprising given the Church was at the heart of medieval society. On the surface, this may appear to be a regression in the development of the historical discipline in that it appears to be guided by faith rather than reason. However, it should be noted that medieval scholars were also wrestling with the new approach of "scholasticism"—the identification of a problem or question and then addressing that issue. In short, scholasticism compelled medieval historians to examine the past, examine the Bible, and then reconcile it with the ancient literature of those like Aristotle. History, although perhaps focused on faith, was becoming more eclectic in its sources and analytical in its

---

Herodotus". *History and Theory* 39 (3) 2000: 384–395; Justin Marozzi, *The Way of Herodotus: Travels with the man who Invented History*. Cambridge, MA: Da Capo Press, 2009; and James Romm, *Herodotus*. New Haven: Yale University Press, 1998.

approach.[13] In fact, it is during this period that one of the world's greatest thinkers, Thomas Aquinas (1225-1274CE) in his work *Summa Theologica* noted the very "subjective" nature of human knowledge. In doing so, he opened up the doors (or re-opened) on the question of historical objectivity.[14] Western European historians and thinker-philosophers were not the only ones wrestling with this subject. Inb Khaldun (1332-1406CE), for example, was a prominent Muslim historian and author of *Mugaddimah*. He established rules for practicing the historical discipline and what he regarded as a "new science."

The Enlightenment Historians

The enlightenment brought us a new period of history. As explorers, in pursuit of wealth and power, began to sail

---

[13] Sayegh and Altice, 9.

[14] Sayegh and Altice, 9. See also Frederick Copleston, *Aquinas: An Introduction to the Life and Work of the Great Medieval Thinker*. New York: Penguin Books, 1991; James Weisheipl, *Friar Thomas D'Aquino: his Life, Thought, and Work*. Garden City, New York: Doubleday, 1974; Fuad Baali, *The Science of Human Social Organization : Conflicting Views on Ibn Khaldun's (1332–1406) Ilm al-umran*. Lewiston,NY: Edwin Mellen Press, 2005; Walter Fischel, *Ibn Khaldun in Egypt : His Public Functions and his Historical Research, 1382–1406*. Berkeley: University of California Press, 1967.

beyond their world's edge, they discovered new worlds beyond their own. Those exploring experiences helped prompt new assessments of the past and how the past was recorded. It didn't refute the traditional Great Chain of Being where God ruled supreme, and then below that white-bearded fellow were the angels and saints, then humans with whites leading the way and men first among them. White men were followed in succession by white women, other races, down to the Blacks and their questionable neighbors, primates. Down through the Great Chain of Being were the mammals, reptiles, amphibians, fishes, insects, plans and so on until we hit, literally, rock bottom. That perspective did not change. But because the world was so much more cluttered, enlightenment thinkers had to develop ways to rationalize the world, reconcile it with the old creation myths (like the Bible) and then order it anew. The ordering process by which enlightenment scholars used was, and has been since, referred to as the "scientific method." Of course, it has evolved over time and glaring problems in its method have been exposed, but the technique remains today in how we analyze things. In short, during this period, historians began to look for more objective evidence. They increasingly demanded proof. The topics remained the same (the elite, the royalty, their wars for power and profit), but the techniques for assembling those stories became more complex. Historians simply did not observe the story anymore or ask around as the ancients often did, but looked to the growing body of literature, government documents, and other primary sources to guide our conclusions. Our social groups had grown to such an extent that it'd become impossible for any one individual to monitor, measure, record, assess and evaluate all the sections from within a group. How they wrote these histories still had a semblance of poetry and literature to them, but they were already en route to the sterile texts of the 20th century. A fundamental shift, however, within enlightenment history, however, was that the folly of history, the seeming unpredictability of events, was no longer ascribed to the Gods or the stars, but to the folly of humans themselves. Niccolo Machiavelli wrote, "Whoever wants to foresee the future must consult the past; for human events ever resemble those of preceding times. This arises from the fact that they are produced by men who have ever been, and ever shall be, animated by the same passions, and thus they necessarily have the same results."[15]

Renaissance historians increasingly returned to the classics. In doing so, this movement led to a humanist approach to history and to a growing lack of interest in using the Divine to explain human events. All of this, naturally, was part of the move toward science and the scientific method.[16] Francis Bacon, for example, in his work, *Novum Organum,* introduced the idea of the scientific method: hypothesis, observation and data, and conclusion.[17]

Renaissance/Enlightenment historians increasingly began to view the past in not only a secular way, but also a

---

[15] Archer, 107. For renaissance historians see Anthony Grafton, *What Was History? The Art of History in Early Modern Europe.* New York: Cambridge University Press, 2007 and Wallace K. Ferguson, *The Renaissance in Historical Thought: Five Centuries of Interpretation.* Boston: Houghton Mifflin, 1948.
[16] Sayegh and Altice, 9.
[17] Sayegh and Altice, 2.

linear way. Their perception of time expanded to that of a linear progression from the heart of ancient civilizations in the Middle East, to Greece and Rome, to western Europe and the modern states, and ultimately to the New World. It was a linear view of the world that attempted to explain (or rationalize) their superiority (or colonial subjugation) over the rest of the planet. Although blossoming in this period, this notion of linear/progressive history has not gone away. Historian Georg W. F. Hegel noted that historical development progressed toward freedom. In his "dialectic", Hegel suggested that between two pendulum points ("thesis" and "antithesis") a struggle existed that led to a new historical point, which he called "synthesis." And, once that synthesis was established as the new "point", a counter "antithesis" was developed and a new struggle ensued with a new synthesis emerging. In doing so, he argued, mankind zig-zagged in a herky-jerky fashion toward progress. Note, however, that while Hegel is suggesting "progress" as the ultimate destination, he is also suggesting that conflict or struggle was the primary mover of history. Adam

Smith suggested a progressive historical development toward

economic improvement. Even Karl Marx, the great bogeyman

for many Americans, used the idea of historical progress toward

communism.[18] Ultimately, the historians' craft itself heeds to a

belief in a progressive movement toward "truth."[19]

19th century Historians and Professionalization

By the 19th century, history as a discipline was

increasingly becoming standardized and professionalized. It

eschewed the values of objectivity and clear analytical thought.

This is both an advancement and a regression, however, for the

---

[18] Sayegh and Altice, 11. See also Corrado Vivanti, *Niccolò Machiavelli: An Intellectual Biography*. Princeton: Princeton University Press: 2013; Frederick Beiser, ed. *The Cambridge Companion to Hegel*. Cambridge: Cambridge University Press, 1993; Frederick C. Beiser, *Hegel*. New York: Routledge, 2005; H. S. Harris, *Hegel: Phenomenology and System*. Indianapolis: Hackett, 1995; Stephen Houlgate, *An Introduction to Hegel. Freedom, Truth and History*. Oxford: Blackwell, 2005; Eric Hobsbawm, *How to Change the World: Tales of Marx and Marxism*. London: Little, Brown, 2011; David McCLellan, *Karl Marx: A Biography*. Hampshire: Palgrave MacMillan, 2006; Peter Singer, *Marx*. Oxford: Oxford University Press, 1980; and Jonathan Sperber, *Karl Marx: A Nineteenth-Century Life*. New York: W. W. Norton & Co., 2013.

[19] Peter Novick, *That Noble Dream: The "Objectivity Question" and the American Historical Profession*. Cambridge: Cambridge University Press, 1988, 4.

discipline. It is an advancement in that historians began to objectively examine subjects, assess and minimize their own bias, and tell the story according to the facts and data revealed. So, unlike some of their predecessors who used stories to validate preconceived notions of a people's superiority or inferiority, these new "modern" historians sought to examine the evidence before forming their own thesis. But, this has unfortunately led some historians and certainly lay observers to conclude that we as historians simply deal with raw facts; that somehow our discipline is guided by "tangible, touchable, unmediated, and raw facts that are put together like puzzle pieces."[20]

This new 19th century historical discipline largely emerged in German universities. Foremost among this new breed of historians was Leopold von Ranke (1795-1886). "In assiduity and scrupulosity of research, in the critical treatment of a wide range of previously unused sources, in the volume of his productivity, and in his development of the seminar for the

---

[20] Sayegh and Altice, 2.

training of scholars, Ranke was unprecedented and unsurpassed."[21] Ranke argued that historians just ought to write what it was and to be objective and clear in what was being told. He argued that historians' task was to report "wie es eigentlich gewesen" (as it actually happened).[22] Today, this appears incredibly naïve. Most of my runny-nosed college freshmen recognize the impossibility of telling what "actually happened." They realize, by virtue of their modern world, that there are no absolutes and that the reporting of what happened hinges on the storyteller. Yet, 19th century historians and their subsequent disciples all increasingly distanced themselves from "history as art" and "history as literature."[23]

---

[21] Novick, 26.

[22] Sayegh and Altice, 14. See also Andreas D. Boldt, *The Life and Work of the German Historian Leopold von Ranke (1795–1886): An Assessment of His Achievements.* Lewiston, NY: Edwin Mellen Press, 2015; Richard Evans, *In Defence of History.* London: Granta Books, 2000; John Farrenkopf, "The Challenge of Spenglerian Pessimism to Ranke and Political Realism," *Review of International Studies*, Vol. 17, (1991)No. 3: 267–284; Peter Gay, *Style In History.* New York: McGraw-Hall, 1974; and Felix Gilbert, "Historiography: What Ranke Meant," *The American Scholar*, Vol. 56, No. 3, 1987: 393–397.

[23] Novick, 40.

American Historians

Americans have long envisioned themselves as an "exceptional people." It was, therefore, not difficult for many American historians to adopt the idea of the linear progressive historical development idea and warp it to their own national design. George Bancroft, for example, argued that the United States was a product of God's will and a product of that never-ending progress.[24] Note, however, that the progression of civilization (as envisioned by these 19th and early 20th century thinkers) was always a westward phenomenon. Americans' faith in progress is one of our nation's hallmark qualities. It is, as Zerubavel has noted, what separates us from "Afghans or Australian aborigines."[25]

But, as some Americans were completely embracing the idea of progress and American exceptionalism, some American historians began to cast doubts on the whole enterprise.

---

[24] Sayegh and Altice, 12-13.
[25] Zerubavel, 15.

Herbert Butterfield and Carl Becker, for example, challenged the assumption that historians were "objective."[26] At the end of the 19th century, for example, when the United States was beginning to accumulate its own empire, some American historians began to question the "real" story behind the American Revolution and the War for Independence. They, now faced with the same imperial dilemmas, began to sympathize with 18th century Britain. This new "Imperial School" was in direct contradiction to American dogma: the Brits were evil oppressors of the liberty-loving Americans and they had no right to tax us, impose restrictions on us, and then militarily occupy "us." The new Imperial School instead offered a new rational approach to understanding our past and it was born out of new contemporary circumstances.[27]

---

[26] Sayegh and Altice, 15.
[27] Novick, 82. See also Carl L. Becker, "Everyman His Own Historian," *The American Historical Review*, Vol. 37, No. 2, 1932.

Marxist Historians

By the 20th century, some historians increasingly found the ideas of Marx and his interpretation of the past (not necessarily his economic views) as a good model for understanding history. Eric Hobsbawm and Howard Zinn are two examples of historians influenced by Marxist history.[28] In short, they saw history through the lens of economic struggle. Like Hegel's "dialectic", Marxist history argued that history was propelled by struggle (in this case economic struggle). It was, they argued, a struggle between the "haves" and "have nots" for the resources of the planet. Marxist historiography emphasizes the role of social class and economic constraints in determining historical circumstances.

---

[28] Sayegh and Altice, 24-25. See also Philip Bounds, "From Folk to Jazz: Eric Hobsbawm, British Communism and Cultural Studies", *Critique: Journal of Socialist Theory*, Vol. 40 No. 4, 2012: 575–593; Norah Carlin and Ian Birchall, "Eric Hobsbawm and the Working Class", *International Socialism*, No.2:21, 1983; J. Cronin,"Creating a Marxist Historiography: the Contribution of Hobsbawm" *Radical History Review*, vol. 19, 1979: 87–109; Gregory Elliott, *Hobsbawm: History and Politics*. London: Pluto Press, 2010; Martin Duberman, *Howard Zinn: A Life on the Left*. New York: The New Press, 2012; David Greenberg, "Agit-Prof: Howard Zinn's influential mutilations of American history," *The New Republic*, March 19, 2013; and Davis D. Joyce, *Howard Zinn: A Radical American Vision*. New York: Prometheus Books, 2003.

This is an important shift, less in terms of the argument they are making, but by certain assumptions included in those decisions. First, these historians maintained their commitment to factual evidence. Yet, and this is the second point, they also understood that the value of history was not only to uphold Ranke's commitment to tell what "actually happened" but to also inform us about our future and thereby shape the future. In short, Marxist and subsequent modern 21st century historians realize that there is a certain level of activism and social change inherent in the new discipline of history.

The New Historians

This is a legitimate title for a school of history still alive today. Over the course of time, it has morphed in and out of different shapes (progressives in the early 20th century, the New Left in the 1960s, and the New Historians of the 1990s) but it is not unreasonable to lump these schools together.[29] It strikes me funny, however, as it is no longer "new" and as historians

---

[29] Novick, 89.

we should have known better to call ourselves by something that will naturally be outdated by something newer. This school is a hodge-podge of diverse approaches that began shortly after the turn of the 20th century. It contains elements and was strongly influenced by the Annales School where not only historical documents were the source of written histories. Instead, they argued, historians ought to examine anthropological evidence, sociological studies, and geography. As a "social constructionist" historian, I clearly myself fall within this school. I have long argued, especially in my examinations of crime and punishment, that one cannot understand the nature of a historical crime and its subsequent societal punishment without understanding the community where that crime was committed; the race, gender, ethnicity of all principals involved; the economics, politics, and geography of the community; and the prevailing sentiment of the people living there. In short, as historians it behooves us to examine every little detail about a community before coming to a conclusion. Yet, we are also painfully aware that "bias" remains a force in our work regardless of how desperately we try to eliminate that subjectivity. I know, for example, that by simply asking questions about criminals and asking how society got them to that point of the offense being committed suggests a bias toward the criminal. It is, by asking the question "how did society create a criminal?", an implication of responsibility on society. Yes, I agree. No subject of inquiry (even within the sciences) can remove itself from the study. A scientist studying a bacteria in a petri dish has already changed the bacteria, has suggested value to that bacteria, and may have already transformed the bacteria by the warmth of his breath, by its isolation in the dish, and god knows what other micro-cosmic affects.

This "new" history is also different in that it has increasingly studied society from the "bottom up."[30] We have long read the histories of the Great White Men and their contributions to society. But, as society changed, we increasingly saw the value of understanding the roles of less

---

[30] Sayegh and Altice, 50.

important individuals (but very important groups). African-Americans, long neglected in American history texts, could no longer be ignored by the 1950s and 1960s. They not only marched in the streets, but they bounded into our history texts. It seems remarkable today, but how on earth could a historian have told the story of the American nation *without* telling the story of the American slave, of the race riots of the 1840s and 1900s? How could we tell the story of this nation while not including half its population—women? How can we tell the story of the American economic machine without telling the experiences of 19th century immigrants, migrant workers in the southwest, and so forth? In short, "new" historians of the late 20th and early 21st centuries could no longer keep that story out.

I am, as a historian, probably a combination of both the New Historian and the Marxist Historian. I am a Marxist, not because of the Socialist label some of my friends have given me, but because I often see the story of our historical past through the lens of economics; a competition for resources; and an exploitation of both the land and the people for the sake of a select few. I am a New Historian in that I often study individuals on the "bottom rungs" of society—criminals—and, that I explain their circumstances and stories through a "social constructionist" approach where I examine as many as the factors possible at play—politics, race, geography, gender, economics, and so forth. My work on crime and punishment in Oregon, for example, suggests that we cannot make a comparative study of communities' crimes because crime and punishment are idiosyncratic and interactive. What I mean here is that crime is unique to each community by virtue of its history, population composition, race, economy, geography, and politics. On the surface, one might think that Eugene, Oregon (between 1875 and 1915) had a greater crime problem than Jacksonville, Oregon because its arrest rates were so significantly higher. But, when we begin to examine what actually happened in those communities we begin to see that Eugene did NOT tolerate crime, but was particularly vigilant in its efforts to suppress crime. So, Eugene arrested more of its citizens. Jacksonville, Oregon was a mining town with a large population of single male miners and a thriving number of

saloons. It had an abundance of criminal activity, but because

the city relied so heavily upon that population, it looked the

other way and tolerated crime in ways that Eugene could not.

My point is this—historians like myself believe that examining

the broad sweep of historical circumstances allows us to

understand the true nature of a particular story rather than

making black-and-white conclusions based on partial

information. Unlike some members of the far right wing media,

historians look for complexity and ambiguity in our

understanding of the world.

Although these disciplines are valuable and mark

fundamental shifts in our discipline, it is a more important to

recognize the changing and different views on what "moves"

history. Is history the story of people moved by their

understanding of the Gods or is it a product of conflict; a story

of the haves versus the have-nots? Is it solely the story of war, greed, and power? To what degree has love played in our historical development and how we see the actions of the people before us? In the end, we may need to even question whether "history" is a useful tool anymore. Do we need historians? Or, do we as a discipline need to change to accommodate the rapidly changing world, not just because of technology, but because of values, proximity, and the means by which we have expressed our message.

The Discipline

Ok, so by this point it's pretty clear—history is more than just names and dates. It is both the concrete and unchanging past and it is a dynamic body of "changing interpretations." But, and here's where I often lose my non-History majors, it is also a professional discipline. From the 1890s to the present, historians have gathered to wrestle with ideas, definitions, and establish standards for the practice of this scientific art. I call it a "scientific art," in part to pay

homage to my undergraduate advisor, Fr. Jeremiah Sullivan, but

also to inform you that "History" possesses qualities that are

"science" based and elements that involve artistry. For

example, as a historian (because of the standards established

years ago by my predecessors) it is essential that I back up my

arguments with evidence, that I corroborate testimony, and

that I use the precision and scrutiny of a scientist to tell the

story. Yet, if you have ever read a science treatise, you will

know how dry and often inaccessible those tracts can be.

Historians, as a result, have the obligation of being artists as

well. It is our imperative to tell this precise and evidence-based

story in an artistic, readable and accessible way. This does not

mean taking artistic liberty and somehow adding purple

elephants into the Battle of Gettysburg. It means using the right

words, descriptive (if not poetic) terms to capture the essence

of the story. For example, in my own writing I have found that

short, quick sentences during the crime scenes within my crime

histories help the reader capture a sense of the speed of action and drama of the crimes transpiring. In the sections where I'm writing about the trials, I might use longer sentences to almost replicate the monotony and drudgery of the American legal system. That may not be art according to the definitions some of my art colleagues might use, but it requires a different approach.

How one approaches the discipline of history is fairly well regulated within the professional historical disciplines. Professional Historians belong to one or more of a variety of professional, regional, and/or topical history organizations. The Organization of American Historians and the American Historical Association are the two premier history professional bodies. They help establish acceptable criteria for programs, curricula, degree standards and the like. While they do not offer accreditation, they are central to the professionalization of our field, protecting our field from corporate or political agendas and our academic freedom, and educating about the value of history.

Historians are different than history teachers and they together are different from "history buffs." I applaud each of those three—historians, teachers, and buffs—for their role in society, but they are different and should not be confused. A historian is a professional scholar, a master of both the primary and secondary literature in their field, an individual well-read in adjacent disciplines or sub-disciplines, and a contributor to the body of knowledge. Those last six words are critical. A historian must write, they must publish or produce something that contributes to the discipline and the larger body of literature. While a "history teacher" may *know* their subject, they may not have read all the literature, understand the nuances of interpretation, and rarely write and contribute a new insight into their area of interest. They are also, unfortunately, limited by the state curriculum whereby legislators tell them what they can and cannot teach. Historians, the bulk of whom are university professors and enjoy the freedom of academic research and expression, are not bound by the same restrictive policies. "History Buffs", on the other hand, are a completely odd breed. In many cases, because of their passion for a detailed subject within history, they are often better informed and more knowledgeable about the specific minutiae of a time period than the historian and history teacher combined. A history buff, for example, might be involved in a historical re-enactment group, know that group's historical whereabouts during the Civil War, and know the exact maker of 1863 regimental uniform buttons. Some historians may know that. Some history teachers may know that. But most of them certainly do not care. It is simply beyond the scope of their interest and/or purpose. It behooves the "history buff" re-enactor to know it because it compels them toward the historical accuracy of their re-enactment. A teacher could care less because they have a greater task of educating the students about the larger phenomenon. The historian cares even less because it hardly makes it into the realm of historical significance and is, therefore, not worthy of their consideration in their interpretation formation process.

Maybe another way to think about what constitutes "history" is to think about through the analogy of my yard. We moved into our home shortly after our arrival in Edinboro. Our backyard stretches some 150+ yards straight back to the east and then does a sort dog-leg to the north. It is 1 ½ acres of yard and wooded area. The front section, closest to the house, is well-manicured yards and garden while the far back (including that dog-leg section) is thickly wooded area with 100 to 150 foot oak trees that stretch along the edge of a gully through which a tributary to French Creek runs. When we bought the house, the property had no fence. The only wat we could determine where our property started and ended was through old markers and a general assessment of what might constitute the divide between the two adjacent properties. Only an old rusty barbed-wire fence gave us any indication of a property-line and it stood at the far eastern end at the bottom of that gully. After a few years, we put in a fence that encompassed all of our property except that gully. We agreed with a neighbor to keep a back tract open to allow students to more easily pass through to the university. But, the property was now fully enclosed. We had three gates—a large two-gated entry at the front, a second large two-gated entry at the rear overlooking the gully, and a third single-gate that accessed to the north. So, here's the analogy. The yard, unencumbered by a fence, represents "history" in general. It is that "concrete past" I referred to earlier because it just was. It was open space. There were no limitations. In theory, one could not determine exactly where it started or where it ended. But, then we put in the fence that represents "interpretations." We interpreted where the yard was, defined it by placing limitations around it (a fence or a label) and called it ours. That fence gave it a new dynamic. Instead of just being "yard" it now became "our yard" to us and "their yard" to them. It bestowed a sense of ownership. There were three accesses to the yard (through the gates) but fewer than had been there before when it was wide open. Lastly, how the yard took shape then represents the discipline of history. As the "owner" of that yard I shaped it in ways suitable to my tastes. I replaced some of the front section of that backyard with a large patio. I added a number of flower gardens and a small arbor. I even added a sizeable vegetable garden further back where we grew beans, arugula, peppers, and tomatoes. I shaped the yard. But, it was always more manicured and maintained the closer you got to the house. The far back and beyond the fence (which was still our property) was much more wild and wooded. In history, we tend to know more about the present and more contemporary or recent history than we do about the distant past and so that too was reflected in my yard. I use this analogy to illustrate the limits on history, but also show that the use of symbolic interpretation can open up new avenues for insight into often complicated ideas.

The Reason

So, the question becomes: why study history? Of course, students will give us a wide variety of answers. They almost invariably say, "So we don't make the same mistakes." One student, as is typically the case in my classroom, will even know the famous quote by George Santayana: "Those who cannot remember the past are doomed to repeat it." Being the cruel professor I am, I always ask them who said that quote. When they fail to identify Santayana, I ask them to repeat the quote. To date, no student has gotten the joke (or at least laughed, I should say). For many then, they believe (or purport to believe) that history's value is to prevent making the same mistakes. I ask them then why we still continue to make the same mistakes. One student, not the same one as before typically, will blurt out, "Because history repeats itself." "Ah," I say, "but does it?" At this point every student in the classroom knows they will probably walk into a trap. I ask, "Is the history of 10 minutes ago like any moment before? Is the war in Afghanistan like anything before?" Ultimately, one brave student will raise their hand, but with caution say "Yes?" Of course, history doesn't repeat itself. That "concrete past" cannot be brought back. It cannot be replicated, duplicated, or re-enacted exactly. Time has swept past us. We do, however, have historical events that in their patterns and circumstances appear to be very similar to one another and that, by virtue of those parallels, can and do serve as important models for understanding the world. This is, again, part of the historicity of the world. Historians, history teachers, and history buffs and others see the world through a historical lens. So, then I ask, "Why do we keep making the same mistakes?" Students begin to nod. "Because, I say, maybe we haven't learned that past well enough. Perhaps we don't take this course as seriously as we ought to. Perhaps we ought to have paid greater attention to Mrs. McGillicuddy and Mr. Potratz." As eminent historian David C. McCullough once wrote, "History is a guide to navigation in perilous times. History is who we are and why we are the way we are."[31]

History is also valuable, as I alluded to earlier, because it informs us as to who we are, how we got to where we are. This is not only true for us as a nation, but also as individuals. Just like its critical for us as citizens to know the origin of the Constitution, the nature of the Civil War, and our history as a

---

[31] Archer, 103.

"melting pot," it is also critical for us to know who we are as members of smaller sub-groups (ethnic communities, states, towns, and clubs) and as individuals. We all have a history. I'd suggest that if we only truly understood one another's personal past, each of our neighbor's individual histories, and the path that brought them to where they are, we would be a kinder and gentler nation. Understanding an individual's history can foster greater empathy and can inspire us to be better people. Understanding our own history can also allow us to forgive that past, forgive the sins that others did in the past so that we can move on. It's almost as if we have to know our past and embrace it in order to shake that past and move out from under its shadow. Years ago, I was given a contract by the Eugene Police Department out in my home state of Oregon. They gave it to me because I was a professional historian with a Ph.D. who had written about the department in the past. They did not hire me necessarily because I was a "good" historian. I am not sure most members of the public would have the ability to discern that. I was hired because the department wanted to "purge" its past. Just about every public institution, in one way or another, has some scandal(s) they have swept under the carpet or some skeletons hidden in some closet. Police departments have a long history of abuses committed from within and the Eugene Police Department was no exception. My hiring was a brave step by that department. In effect, they said, "Let's hire someone to dig into our past and tell our story...no restrictions." I did that as best I could. I will admit, I am absolutely positive that not all records were made available to me and that many scandals went untouched. Yet, the department's effort is telling. It suggests that at that time they needed to "purge" that past in order to "move forward." Whether they did or not is not within the subject of this work. In short, owning and embracing our past allows us to break from that past.

I've seen this phenomenon in my own life. My dad was not a very good father (at least to me). But, when I became a father, I was acutely aware of his "fathering." In response to my past, I tried to be different than that past. I tried to show and express my love for my daughters in every possible way. I did not abuse them. I treated them as I wished I had been treated.

But there's the rub. Even when we try to escape "the past,"

that "past" is affecting us and shaping our decisions.

I ask my students "How many of you are historians?"

and, naturally, no one raises their hands. I act puzzled and then

re-phrase the question. "Let me ask it this way," I say, "how

many of you are historical thinkers?" Yet again, no one raises

their hand. "No one?" I say in mock surprise. "Hmm," I

continue, "so how many of you walked into this classroom and

stopped?" I stand in front of the class before an empty chair. I

look at the chair, examine it from every possible angle, and then

with caution I touch the seat of the chair. "What is this?" I say.

"What *is* this? *What* is this? What is *this?*" I circle the chair and

slowly, ever-cautious, lower my butt into the chair and as I do

so, I say, "Whatever it is, it fits my ass perfectly. Perfect, almost

as if it were designed just for this purpose. What is it? What do

you call it?" I quickly stand and ask again, "How many of you

came in this morning and did that?" No one raises their hand.

"Of course not," I say, "that's because you are all historical thinkers. None of you have done anything without using the past as a guide in one way or another. You sat in your chairs because you remembered that in almost all the cases in the past, these things called "chairs" have been used for sitting and have sufficiently supported your weight. You got here today because you remembered the route you took here. You took that route because you remembered you had class. You came to this university based on a whole host of memories and decisions. You came here because your parents sacrificed for you to get here, their grandparents got off the boat or were freed as slaves and sacrificed to get you here." Memories and history and decisions and the brain are all wrapped up together and to act like they are different is to ignore those facts and deny our role in the historical process. It is a denial of our importance in that history.

History is *NOT* names and dates. That is important. We certainly need to know who were important characters and the chronology of events, but it's not what is central to the lesson. Historians and teachers and history buffs will know, need to know, and know how to know names and dates, but is it central

to what we want? Is it central to the value of history? Are the

dates critical to our understanding of any story or might a

simple understanding of chronological order be sufficient? I

first noticed the lump in my leg on February 4, 2013. Dr.

Clemente first examined it on February 19, 2013. The biopsy

was done on March 14, 2013 and I was diagnosed on March 22,

2013. On May 7, 2013, Drs. Lietman and Saverino at the

Cleveland Clinic removed the tumor and most of my left femur.

I was released on March 15, 2013. I am, as I write this, laid up in

bed rest. Do the specific dates matter so much as the

chronology? I discovered it, sought medical treatment, had it

removed, and now live. Someday, they will add some dates to

the end. His cancer returned and he died. But the central

importance lay not in the specific dates, but in the chronology.

It's the story. Now, when historians unearth events of the past,

they need to be aware of specific dates so that *they* can get the

story's chronology right. After that, however, I wonder if it's

really that critical. I wonder that because the value of history is to know who we are, where we came from, and who (as a result) we want to be.

Unfortunately, over the course of the late 19th century and the entire 20th century, historians have searched for the ultimate scholarly Holy Grail: Objectivity. We praise it, think we are practicing it, but never realize that "noble dream."[32] As the great historian Peter Novick has noted, historians vow to "purge themselves of extended loyalties."[33] Objectivity, as Novick defines it, "include a commitment to the reality of the past, and to truth as correspondence to that reality; a sharp separation between knower and known, between fact and value, and, above all, between history and fiction." Those who have faith in "Objectivity" posit that there is and must be a distinction between what happened (the fact) and how we twist and manipulate it as human beings AND that the historical fact is of prime importance. It, this faith in objectivity, has become a "scientistic cult."[34] The problem with this is not as Novick

---

[32] Novick, Title.
[33] Novick, 2.
[34] Novick, 42.

describes, that "objectivity" (and its pursuit) has become falsely equated with "authoritative."[35] Instead, the problem is that "objectivity" has removed the human folly out of the equation. It has removed the art, the literature of the writing. It has taken the timbre out of the storyteller's voice and the animated gestures away from the shaman-poet. What made history so valuable was its ability to connect to other humans in the present and that special elan that was celebrated in our past historians' versions has now been abandoned. In 1892, at a history teaching conference future President of the United States and History PhD Woodrow Wilson said, "we must avoid introducing what is called scientific history in the schools, for it is a 'history of doubt,' criticism, examination of evidence. It tends to confuse pupils." No, Mr. President, you are quite wrong.[36] Teaching our students critical thinking skills is absolutely necessary in this world. The problem, again, is not

---

[35] Novick, 51.

[36] Let's also just state for the record that Wilson was the same historian (and president) who gave a ringing endorsement of the landmark film *Birth of a Nation* despite its glorification of the KKK and racist stereotypes.

the "science" or this belief that science is objective. The problem is that we need to make sure that our students, despite the science, still see the magic, the mystery, the awe of the human past. And, perhaps, there is nothing wrong with having an agenda in one's scholarly intent. Perhaps the world needs that. Frederick Jackson Turner, one of the discipline's greats, once wrote that "each age writes the history of the past anew with reference to the conditions uppermost in its own time."[37] But, unfortunately, as we all pretend to be objective, we continue on our own biased paths marking out a new historical trajectory. Yet, even as we fall to the inevitable fate of subjectivity, we have foolishly removed the elements in our works that make them lively, inspiring, and provocative. In doing so, we have seen the consequences, an "erosion of historians' popular audience." From the 1950s to the present, historians write in such a stifled way that the only ones who would want (or dare) to read our works are other historians. If that's the case then have we not become simply antiquarians?

---

[37] Novick, 103.

Are we no better than the little old lady at the county historical society collecting dusty spoons? We archive our thoughts and no change comes from them. This strikes me as a profession of which I'd rather NOT be a part. Instead, I want my students and my readers to be informed and enlightened, but also inspired and radicalized. I'd like them to be so provoked that they take action against an injustice, stand up for their rights, and become part of the national fabric. Moreover, I'd like my students to understand the "other." I'd like them to empathize with people of the past and thereby become more empathetic to their neighbors. Admittedly, I am an associate of the Sisters of St. Joseph. Our charism (as both nuns and their lay associates) is "neighbor with neighbor, neighbor with God, without distinction." That spiritual mission and my academic philosophy means that I have an obligation to reach my students to make them better people, not simply warehouses of facts, names and dates. John Womack was reported to have said, "Teaching about pain...is the most important thing history can do."[38] I concur. The pain of our past will remedy our future.

Let's remind ourselves that the historians of today were

the poets of yesteryear and the shamans before them. As

ancient tribes, we moved across the land hunting and gathering

and as we stopped each night, we might ask an elder (a

shaman) to tell our story and tell us how we came to be.

Through oral tradition that elder told "creation stories" or

"origin myths" that creatively wove together their primitive

understanding of the universe, the stars, life and death, and

from whom and where they came. With the development of

writing, the leaders began writing down the stories of their

ascendancy, their ties to the past and legitimacy to govern the

present. In the time of the Greeks and Romans, historians

wrote about wars and thinkers and leaders. That style and

focus, in many ways, remained until the 20th century. Today,

historians are not shamans. The role of the shaman has since

been divided among priests, physicians, poets, psychologists,

and historians. This is, perhaps, an unfortunate development.

Perhaps our spiritual character craves the past; our bodies need

---

[38] Novick, 462.

that connection; our art needs to be more infused with it and History needs humanization. The new history shaman, however, needs memory and dreams to guide him or her. Thus, history is again tied to memory and dreams...the import of this work.

CHAPTER TWO

Memory and the Survival of the Species

Introduction

So, I have been blessed with a great memory. It may be genetic, but I doubt that explains it entirely. I believe I have a good memory (and we'll explore this more here in a few pages) because I have trained my brain to remember better.[39] I have always remembered things and I have always tried to remember better. I have used a variety of techniques and tricks and, in doing so, I believe I have trained my brain to remember new things more easily. In short, I believe that through practice you can re-hardwire your brain in such a way that new things that you want to "remember" can be better remembered. For example, when I began teaching I believed it was critical to know my students' names. How can I expect them to do well in

---

[39] It is worth noting here that "memory" refers or measures what we can "retrieve" from our brain not so much what we have "stored" in our brain. Howard Bloom, *Global Brain: The Evolution of Mass Mind from the Big Bang to the 21st Century.* New York: John Wiley and Sons, Inc., 2000, 99.

the class if I can't hold them accountable by name and hold them to that higher standard? Moreover, I believe knowing my students' names is a sheer matter of respect. So, that first time I saw the class roster in advance of the first day of class, I studied their names and studied their names. When the first day of class rolled around, I had them turn in a sheet of paper with their names and other information on it. I called it my "Student Information" form and I used it as an excuse to have a face-to-face encounter with the student. Their names had already been drilled into my brain, I now only had to attach that name to a face. I then proceed to go row by row and name the students without using any cheat sheets or class roster. I occasionally hit a stumbling block, but I generally got anywhere from 70% to 95% correct. Most students were generally surprised. I told them that my memory was not a "gift," but a "skill." I practiced. I also told them that if they thought my memory of their names was creepy that they should not worry. If they found me outside their dorm window, however, I told them to call the campus police. It was not a "gift." I practiced remembering. I fired the synapses in my brain enough times that I could re-fire them at will. I later found that the amount of time I used to "train my brain" went down over the course of my years doing this exercise. In short, my brain got so good at remembering students' names that each time I had to do it, I used less time to get it accomplished. By the way, I once had a student who enrolled in one of my classes and was subject to my name-recall exercise on the first day of class, but then dropped the course. Years later, I came across this student in public and was able to call her by name. She stood stupefied. I could not bear to tell her that I remembered her name because she shared her last name with a rodent. So, if you have bought this book and you ultimately seek my signature in the front cover; and if, in that process, you tell me your last name is "Monkeybutt", I'm pretty sure I'm going to remember your name and that book signing event *forever*. We'll address why that occurs later within this chapter.

The fact of the matter, however, is this: we teach our kids to "practice" their musical instruments if they want to be successful and play music; we teach our kids to "practice" their sports if they want to be successful on the court or field or mats; BUT, we rarely ask our kids to "practice" using their brains. As an aside, I believe my own daughters' tremendous academic success in life was that they *did* practice using their brains. They always had paper and pencils available. They always had books at their fingertips. They had parents who actively role-modeled learning through reading, writing, and research. Memory is a skill. We have it naturally as part of a human make-up, but its strength hinges on our ability to use it, to use regularly, and to use it effectively. Our brains will probably store the memories whether we like it or not. But, it's our ability to tap into those memories that becomes essential for our survival. "To be useful," Eric Kandel, a famous neuroscientist once wrote, " a memory has to be recalled. Memory retrieval depends on the presence of appropriate cues that an animal can associate with its living experience." [40] The memory needs to be tapped.

---

[40] Eric Kandel, *In Search of Memory: The Emergence of a New Science*

The Past

Our understanding of memory in the past was grossly incorrect. In their defense, however, given the level of science, how were we to know? Memory is now the subject of psychologists and neuroscientists and although great headway has been made in the last 50 years, we still have a long way to go. In fact, I'd argue that this kind of study (study of brain and memory) is truly our "Last Frontier" and is more important o human development and our species' survival than anything else done—so thank you neuroscientists!

In the past, we thought of memory according to our human earthly ways of ordering our world. So, when we thought of memory and we tried using our memory in the pre-historic days and ancient eras, we looked to the stars, to the environment, and we created mental maps in our head. Much like what a goose might do for its trip back to the Canadian north. It uses its memory of the landscape to connect to

of Mind. New York: W. W. Norton and Co., 2006, 215.

another landmark and then proceeds to it, looking for the next geographic feature which triggers the next. Human memory, like that of a goose en route to Ontario, never takes a direct route, but meanders over the terrain until it finds its final destination.

In the enlightenment era, we began to order our new world (in the Great Chain of Being). We ordered our world in encyclopaedia, in catalogs and lists. Likewise, humans began to think of their own memory as a "card catalog" as if the brain was neatly ordered alphabetically with easy to use corss-references that would link us to another text, another idea and so on. Even today, when I watch students trying to remember things during a test, I will catch them fiddling through an imaginary catalog in their head, their hands literally maneuvering through thin air at the base of their forehead. But memory is obviously much more complex than a card-catalog system. How would one explain the random memories we dredge up were that the case? Clearly, my stepping on a nail in a filbert orchard in Oregon as a smail child has little to do with

Syria's use of chemical weapons, but the two thoughts came up one after another.

Thankfully, those remarkable neuroscientists have done landmark work and have begun to break through those misconceptions. In the end, however, we must all admit—it's ALL memory. Tennessee Williams in his work, "The Milk Train Doesn't Stop Here Anymore," wrote: "Has it ever struck you…that life is all memory, except for the one present moment that goes by so quickly you hardly catch it going? It's really all memory…except for each passing moment."[41] If all life is sheer memory and the brain is the repository of memory, then the brain is also the repository of life. Therefore, our understanding and our quest for the "meaning of life" hinges on memory, the brain, and all that contributes to those mental functions, including dreams. Again, I ask my students are "historians" and none of them raise their hands. I then ask them, "how many of you are historical thinkers?" and only a few raise their hands. I ask them a third question, "how many of you remember?" and

---

[41] Kandel, 281.

all of their hands shoot into the air. "Almost every reality you 'know' at any given second is a mere ghost held in memory."[42] Memory is, as Howard Bloom has noted, "the core of what we call reality."[43]

The Process

The process of the memory is complex and even the top neuroscientists will today attest that they have only begun to scratch the surface in understanding how the human memory operates. It is not surprising that memory has often been called the "Holy Grail of neuroscience."[44] To understand the basics of memory, it is therefore critical for us to have a shared rudimentary understanding of the brain.

The brain is complex—now that's an understatement. It has "distinct information-processing systems for filtering out distractions, learning skills, controlling the body, remembering

---

[42] Bloom, 72.
[43] Bloom, 72.
[44] V. S. Ramachandran and Sandra Blakeslee, *Phantoms in the Brain: Probing the Mysteries of the Human Mind.* New York: Harper Perennial, 1998, 148.

facts, holding information temporarily, and storing and executing rules."[45] These divergent tasks, however, are all centered around "memory" in one way or another. So, the question then remains—how does all of this happen?

When one thinks about it, it truly is amazing. We, as humans, have the capability of recalling events and images from the distant past, hold them within "our mind's eye" and then do with those memories as we see fit. We can create analogies to those mental images, draw lessons from them, infer certain cause and effect relationships and so on. All "thinking" as we know it draws in one way or another from our ability to remember. We survive because of memory. It is as neuroscientist Douglas Hofstadter once said a "miracle of self-reference."[46] It behooves us then to quickly remind ourselves (as we know it today) how the brain works and how memory operates within that entangled web of mystery.

---

[45] Steven Pinker, *The Blank Slate: The Modern Denial of Human Nature*. New York: Penguin Books, 2002, 40.
[46] Douglas Hofstadter, *I am a Strange Loop*. New York: Basic Books, 2007, 363.

Memory, as we now know it, is not centrally located in just one section or portion of the brain. Memory, in fact, involves a variety of coordinated efforts by different parts of the brain. The prefrontal cortex, for example, is the "seat" of the "self-conscious" and plays an important role in the mind's processing.[47] The fronto-parietal regions in the brain are also very active metabolically even at rest because they're consolidating details of our personal history, as if in a "covert journal." This will not only be a critical region for our ability to remember, but also a critical region for our dreaming, to which we will return later.[48]

The process of memory also involves the movement of information from its short-term storage area into long-term memory. This process is known as "consolidation."[49] Short-

---

[47] Bruce Lipton, *The Biology of Belief: Unleashing the Power of Consciousness, Matter, and Miracles.* Carlsbad, CA: Hay House, Inc., 2005, 184.

[48] James H. Austin, *Selfless Insight: Zen and the Meditative Transformations of Consciousness.* Cambridge: M.I.T. Press, 2009, 71. "The first suggestion that some aspects of human memory can be stored in specific regions of the brain arose in 1948 from Penfield's neurological work." Kandel, 125. Wilder Penfield (1891-1976) was a pioneer neuroscientist in the memory field. Unfortunately, for most Americans, his name is largely forgotten. Ironic.

term memories are converted to long term in the region of the

brain known as the hippocampus and are then stored back in

the original areas of perception, the pre-frontal cortex.[50]   It is

worth noting here that unconscious memory "resides outside

the hippocampus and the medial temporal lobe."[51] And,

implicit memories (those dealing with skills, habits, and

conditioning) are stored in the cerebellum, striatum, and

amygdala.[52] This is all worth noting because "memory" resides

in almost every corner of the brain in one way or another. The

idea of localization, introduced after Paul Broca's landmark

1861 discovery, suggests that certain areas of the brain serve

specific functions.   That doctrine has been largely disproven,

but has been central to even 21st century thinkers about the

brain.[53]

---

[49] Kandel, 199-210. In the 19th century, Muller and Alfons Pilzecker
believed memory took time to fixate or, in their term,
"konsoldierung."
[50] Kandel, 130.
[51] Kandel, 129.
[52] Kandel, 130.
[53] Mark R. Rosenzweig and Edward L. Bennett, *Neural Mechanisms of Learning and Memory*. Cambridge: MIT Press, 1976, 4,5, 14

But to understand the power and process of memory, we need to look beyond the basic anatomy and sections of the brain. In short, the brain is comprised of millions and millions of neurons. Neurons are simply nerve cells. The cell body itself is covered by a double layer of lipid (or fat-like) molecules and is a permeable substance that allows some things in and not others. The cell itself is filled with cytoplasm, a jelly-like substance, that contains mitochondria that breaks down nutrients having entered the cell and converts those nutrients, like glucose, into energy for the cell. The cells also have two important features called dendrites and axon terminals. Dendrites extend from the cell body and serve as "receptors" for the cell. The axon is a long shaft protruding from the cell. Covered with a myelin sheath, at the end of which are a series of terminals that serve as "projectors." In short, neurons communicate with one another through these "receptors" and "projectors." But let's be clear, it 's NOT the neuron itself that "houses" the memory. As Kandel notes, "...the cellular mechanisms of learning and memory reside not in the special properties of the neuron itself, but in the connections it receives and makes with other cells in

the neuronal circuit to which it belongs."[54] In the same way

that a building is not defined in its shape by the beams that

make it up, learning and memory are not *in* the neuron. The

building (and memory) are defined by the multiplicity of

connections between beams (and neurons). This is not to

minimize the role of the neuron. In fact, in a belief known as

the "Neuron Doctrine," most scholars agree that the neuron is

the "fundamental building block and elementary signaling unit

in the brain."[55]

Now, before we move on and more fully address the

process by which neurons communicate, it is worth noting here

that there are different types of neurons. There are, for the

sake of this discussion, three types: sensory neurons,

interneurons, and motor neurons. "Sensory neurons" are

responsible for the reception of sensory input entering into the

brain. They will, of course, be largely located in the sensory

---

[54] Kandel, 142.
[55] Kandel, 59.

sections of the brain. "Motor neurons" are those nerve cells responsible for the movement of the body and the contraction of muscles. "Interneurons" are the translator nerve cells that can communicate between the two other cells. So, let's now return to the process itself. Imagine you are sitting at the edge of a skating rink and a big hulking man comes and takes a baton and smashes your kneecap. Apart from making you angry at the people Tonya Harding has surrounded herself with, you're most likely going to cry and grip your bludgeoned knee in pain. But, here's how it worked in your brain in simplified form: sensory neurons (one or more) received a message through their "receptor" dendrites that a painful event occurred; then, an electrical impulse (generated in the cell from the exchange and displacement of protein anions, chloride ions, potassium ions, and sodium ions from the outside and inside of the cell membrane and its subsequent electrostatic pressure) is sent down the axon through a corresponding chemical reaction. The sensory neuron has successfully received the message and has now transmitted it via the axon terminal "projectors" to the interneuron. The interneuron undergoes a similar electro-chemical process and transmits the message to the Motor Neurons and, using the same electro-chemical process, re-conveys that message back to the muscle cells for the requisite physical reaction: jerking back in horror, swelling, grabbing the knee in pain, and so forth. All of this takes less than seconds to occur, but involves a complex neural communication between hundreds, if not thousands, of nerve cells in the body and thousands of synaptic firings.[56] Neurons communicate with one another at specialized sites between dendrites and terminals, areas known as "synapses." Poor Nancy Kerrigan was afire with electro-chemical communication when she kept crying out, "Why? Why?"

But, let's now step back and make this story a little more complex. We began the scenario above with a sensory input and we begin ALL our thoughts and actions with sensory

---

[56] The science of the brain is still relatively new. For instance, it was not until 1955 that Sanford Paley and George Palade first demonstrated a synaptic cleft between terminal and dendrites of two communicating cells. We had the ability to detonate atomic bombs and harness atomic energy a decade before we understood how our own brains functioned. Kandel, 69.

input. Yet, as Le Doux in *The Emotional Brain* has noted, sensory signals do not go directly to the sensory cortex. Instead, sensory signals first bypass that sensory cortex and go directly to the amygdala. This is all occurring before we even have a chance to be aware of the sensory input. This "so-called 'lower' route begins to make meaning of our experience before we have begun to understand it."[57] Moreover, because the amygdala is responsible for the "fight or flight" response, it is possible that this early way-station for our sensory input is our body and brain's early detection system for danger. I'd further argue that what we often call "intuition" in precarious moments is, in fact, this "lower" route in action.[58]

Just about everything we do, in one way or another, involves that neural process. Input comes in, our body responds, and we move on waiting for the next barrage of stimuli. Please note, we are rarely given the opportunity to experience just one single bit of sensory input. Typically, we are

---

[57] Zull, 59.
[58] Gift of Fear

bombarded with stimuli. For example, if I were to simply stop typing right now, I would undoubtedly experience a whole host of sensory information. So, hold on for a second...............ok, done. In just one minute of motionless observation, I heard different types of birds in my Edinboro backyard, the melting snow drip off the roof, passing cars, the hum of our refrigerator, and the snore of my 17-year old greyhound. I saw the hibiscus plant abloom in my window, my own hands resting on the laptop, and scattered before me. I felt the warmth of the laptop on my DC Comics pajama bottoms, my left big toe resting on the coffee table, and a cool air cross the top of my chemo-balding head. All of these and even more subconsciously perceived sensations were all taken into my brain and registered via these important brain nerve cells. But, let's be clear: memory and thought is not a "place" or stored in some card-catalog fashion in our heads. Thought and memory are processes. It the "persistent change in the relationship between neurons."[59] Forgetting, therefore, is not a loss of

---

[59] Larry Squire, *Memory and Brain.* New York: Oxford University

information, but a decline in persistence. The synaptic connections weakened as they were fired less frequently and at some point became either non-existent or so weak that they could not be fired upon will.[60]

So, this how our brain works (in obviously simplified fashion). But, is it memory? "What we call memory consists of changes in connections between neurons in the brain that cause us to respond in a particular ways to particular stimuli."[61] Different memories are stored in different places. For example, O'Keefe and Dostrovsky, neuroscientists, have demonstrated that neuron activity in the hippocampus is heightened when an animal explores its environment. In short, we have not only "working memory," "episodic memory," and "reference memory" but also "spatial memory" and so on. "Episodic memory" is of particular importance to us historians. "Episodic memory is our private storehouse of episodes that have

Press, 1987, 7.
[60] Squire, 38.
[61] Neil R. Carlson, *Foundations of Physiological Psychology*. Boston: Allyn and Bacon, Inc., 1988, 367.

happened to us and to our friends and to characters in novels we've read and movies we've seen and newspaper stories and TV news clips, and so on, and it forms a major component of the long-term memory that makes us so human."[62] What makes this of such great importance to us as historians is that the entire human record, as we know it, rests in one way or another upon this episodic memory. We rely on individuals to accurately document official records, to register accurate information, and to share accurate descriptions of their own experiences in the formation of these "primary documents." Yet, it's clear from what Douglas Hofstadter said, these memories come from a whole host of sources—some reliable, most not-so-reliable. Have we, in fact, created a fictional past based on the fictional memory of the planet's occupants? Moreover, we know that the human body is hardwired toward sympathy. It is for that reason that when we watch "America's Greatest Bloopers" we cringe when we see a little girl hit her father between the legs with a bat; or a boy skateboarding on

---

[62] Hofstadter, 85.

crashing; or a man flipping off a trampoline and through the family's sliding glass door. We have that built-in sympathy and those sympathetic experiences are stored in our memory, even though they were not OUR experiences.

What we know, however, is that certain neural connections are stronger than others. I doubt that for Nancy Kerrigan the links between the sensory neurons, interneuron, and motor neurons for that particular 1994 affair are very weak. But, presumably we all have weaker connections. But, because of the trauma associated with that event, the importance of the bludgeoning to her career, the attention she immediately received, and the media focus on the attack, her neural connections for that event are strong. As a result, her memory for that event is also strong. We also know that the activity of a synapse (space between neurons) on a particular neuron strengthens the effectiveness of the other. In a process known as "heterosynaptic facilitation" when a synapse changes in size the number of neurotransmitter receptor sites also increases and new terminal buttons develop. [63] In short, one strong memory may, in fact, strengthen other associated memories. The attack on Nancy Kerrigan did not directly involve Tonya Harding. It was a man, after all, who wielded the retractable baton. Yet, in Nancy Kerrigan's memory, Tonya Harding is explicitly linked. Some nerve cells have nearly 50 dendrite branches reaching off them.[64]

So, the brain is constantly working and, as part of its central function, is storing information in a complex multi-layered web so that we can retrieve that information for some purpose. All of that retrieval is, of course, at a later time. "Memory, defined in general terms, refers to the effects of experience that are manifest at a later time."[65] But there are distinctions. Some memories relate to facts and some memories are associated with skills. For that reason, neuroscientists and memory experts have distinguished different memory tropes. Some emphasize the difference

---

[63] Carlson, 388.
[64] Kandel, 65.
[65] James L. McGaugh, Norman N. Weinberger, and Gary Lynch. *Brain Organization and Memory: Cells, Systems, and Circuits*. New York: Oxford University Press, 1990, 23.

between facts, skills, and space. Others distinguish memories according to the types of "records" they refer to: declarative, procedural, conceptual, and episodic.[66]

Once one understands how the brain works and even comprehends the simplest ideas about memory, we can begin to employ the brain to our greater advantage. We know that repetition of a "thought" strengthens the axon and synaptic connections and makes that "thought" more easily accessible. This is critical for our digestion of information, particularly in a history class where students seem overwhelmed with names and dates and all the minutiae that make up our discipline. But, it is also valuable in our ability to reach students. If we understand that certain synaptic connections are stronger than others then maybe we ought to appreciate more where our students came from. It was not that their minds weren't working, but that their minds were forming stronger

---

[66] Michaela Gallagher, "Introduction" in McGaugh, Weinberger, and Lynch, 24; John Anderson (1995) as quoted in James P. Byrnes, *Minds, Brains, Learning: Understanding the Psychological and Educational Relevance of Neuroscientific Research.* New York: The Guiford Press, 2001, 50.

connections in areas we don't necessarily perceive. A student, who we will call "Jimmy," is in college for the first time and is there by virtue of a special admissions process to help the under-prepared. Jimmy grew up on the gritty streets of Philadelphia, he knows how to survive on those streets, and, unfortunately, had some synaptic connections reinforced that told him he was worthless, unsalvageable, and a waste of human space. It is our obligation to teach him regardless of his past. It is my obligation to help him re-wire his thinking, loosen those negative synaptic connections by offering him new connections, new life, and new value to what he is putting in his head.

The Art

When it is all said and done, the brain processes all our sensory input. It collects and archives (for lack of a better word) all the sensations we receive, many of which we are not even aware. When we look through our car's windshield and assess the oncoming traffic and such, we may only consciously and cognizantly "remember" a few details---the blue car that swerved, the child playing curbside, the signs, and so on. Yet, our eyes have seen it "all". Our eyes scanned and imprinted into our heads all of the visual landscape. Once inside the brain, however, as already noted, the brain performed its own form of triage and sent some "facts" (some of the visual imprints) into the mental wastebasket. Yet, we had them at some point. The brain does this with all sensory inputs, but it also wrestles with the warped interpretations we affix to certain images, sounds, and sensations. The brain also processes the "semifictional realities of our own life story." In short, as we age our memories twist and contort to what we *want* them to be. We construct our own past and our memories conform to that new artificially fabricated existence. The great Austrianpsychologist Alfred Adler posited that one's interpretation of early memories was critical. He argued that those memories served as the foundations for our own "private logic" and as metaphors for our subsequent lifestyles.[67] Guy de Maupassant once wrote,

"We are accustomed to use our eyes only with the memory of what other people before us have thought about the object we are looking at."[68] In short, we have sensory input that comes directly from the outside world to our brain, but our understanding of that input has already been shaped by our community of supporters who have taught us, labeled the items, and ascribed certain values to the items we will subsequently see. I may see the corn on the plate just as you do, but my sensory input triggers the memory of my grandfather referring to corn as "pig's food." In the end, we see very different items: human food or pig food. It is this malleability of the brain and human memory that most neuroscientists refer to as its "plasticity." For decades now, despite popular human conception, neuroscientists have been abandoning the idea that there is a "fixed nature of connections in the adult human brain." Instead, "memories are constantly remodeled."[69]

---

[67] Adler (AAD), 58-59.
[68] Bloom, 71.
[69] Norman Doidge, *The Brain that Changes Itself: Stories of Personal*

The Reason

The art of memory is critical for a variety of reasons. First and foremost, without memory we would cease to function as human beings and as societies. There are a whole host of films out there that detail (in serious and not-so-serious ways) the debilitating effects of memory loss. If you haven't seen *Groundhog Day*, please do. Amnesia and other memory loss disorders are crippling. Imagine waking up and not knowing where you were, what was to unfold for you that day, and how you'd survive. It would, for all intents and purposes, slam us back into a primordial state where we have to re-invent and re-discover everything. There is no innate diet. We learned what we can and cannot put into our mouths from both the infant practice of putting everything in our mouths and the

Triumph from the Frontiers of Brain Science. New York: Penguin Books, 2007, 224-229. Let this also be a shout out to Sigmund Freud who seemed to get so much completely wrong when he offered up his idea of the "plastic view of memory."

instructions we received from our parents. The loss of memory

would cripple us in such simple ways. And, let's not forget that

almost every piece of information technology develop)ed over

the course of time was developed to enhance humans' ability to

maintain a better memory. Writing was, after all, developed as

a technology to aid in the count of material goods. Early

cuneiform centered around lists of goods, both those traded

and in surplus, within the kingdom. In short, humans have good

memories, but to ask an individual (like the poor clerk

responsible for maintaining the warehouse for some Sumerian

king) to remember in his head the full inventory of an empire

was simply too much. So, some smart individual came up with

the idea of scratching some symbols down (whether it was in

the mud or on papyrus or one the skin of a ripe watermelon)

that represented the numbers and items within that inventory.

That initial writing was a memory cue. Subsequent writing,

including what we now know as literature, were written down

because no shaman or priest could conceivably remember

EVERY creation myth or story. So, they became writers and

used that to aid in their memory of those stories about their past. In the end, computers and the like have all been modifications of that very early memory technology---all designed to assist us in remembering, knowing, thinking, and analyzing about who we are and who we have been.

In 1979, a scholar named Ingvar theorized that memory was central to an individual's construction of "alternate hypothetical behavior patterns in order to be ready for what may happen."[70] Ingvar was right, but wasn't that exactly what my students (and students long before my own) had argued. Memory allows us to think about patterns of behavior, real, past, fictional and the like, all in order to make better decisions for the future. Memory made history, memory makes the present.

But the value of memory goes well beyond sheer survival. In short, we cannot make critical decisions in ANY discipline without mastery of the facts. I ask my students (and

---

[70] Karl K. Szpunar, et al, "Memories of the Future: New Insights Into the Adaptive Value of Episodic Memory," *Frontiers in Behavioral Neuroscience,* 2013 7;47, 1.

here it is a trick question) "What topic do you want to research?" and they inevitably answer with a wide variety of research topics, from the medieval Church to Vietnam. I then ask them "what's your thesis going to be?" and only a few of them will not raise their hands. Most students simply do not yet fathom that they cannot form a thesis (or a conclusion) until they have examined the evidence. Some of the students naturally had preconceived ideas about their topics, but they still had not collected the evidence, mastered that evidence (learned it, memorized it) such that they could form a reasonable, rational thesis. This is true in all disciplines. I had my tumor removed in May 2013 at the Cleveland Clinic. My physician was an orthopedic oncologist named Steven Lietman. He is one of the top physicians in his discipline and has published multiple scholarly articles on the subject of soft-tissue sarcomas. As an academic, I am particularly attracted to experts, as I think we all should be. Lietman knew his stuff. I would never have tolerated some schmuck who did not know the names of bones and muscles, who had flunked Anatomy and Physiology class, or a surgeon who could not name the tools they were going to use to extract the tumor and cut out the adjacent femur. That would be ridiculous. Memory and memorization are therefore critical to a physician and surgeon's success. Now, having said that, it is also worth noting that not all information is readily available. For example, Dr. Lietman knew his stuff and knows his anatomy and knows soft-tissue sarcomas. But, there was no way for him to know exactly what he was facing until he cut me open. X-rays, biopsies, CT scans, and ultrasounds can only reveal so much. But, given his expertise and his mastery of previous details and the fact that I am an average human being, I had great confidence that my body and my tumor would be close enough to what he had approximated. With a strong memory, memorization, and mastery of detail, Lietman was able to make any necessary adjustments. As a result, he successfully removed both the tumor and the left femur. And memory was central.

So, what is this "memory" really good for? Is it really just for survival? Is it so we can recall caches of food and primal techniques? If so, then aren't we simply like the other animals on the planet, playing to instinct?

No. Our memories are laden with other memories and that multi-layered, complex and nuanced thing we call a "memory" is, in fact, all explicitly tied back to us and to our own identity. When I answer (or ask) the question "Who Am I?", I am drawing upon thousands upon thousands of memories. That might be the central question. It's certainly a question we began this work with and that all disciplines are ultimately asking. But now we know it is what all human life is built around. Yet, each memory contributes to that.

Think of it this way—what is the central value of most institutions (formal or informal)? The most basic human institution might be the relationship between a man and a woman (or between two men or between two women), an institution we broadly call "marriage." Yet, marriage itself is often misunderstood and the relationship has changed over the course of time—from one defined by economic utility to one characterized equally by love and divorce. We've often characterized it as *the* institution that induces procreation and protects the children born from that relationship. In doing so, it helps sustain the viability of the child. In short, a paleo-baby could not have survived in the hostile world into which it was born without protection from its parents (long past the neo-natal nine months) until the child itself is a viable adult. No. Lots of children survived and will continue to survive our hostile world—it may not be ideal to most, but it can work. Communities can and have done just that. BUT, what marriages do for us, perhaps like no other institution, is preserve and perpetuate our memory.

We all want to avoid death, but we know it's coming. As I sit here facing it squarely on another set of bad news, bad CT scans, growing tumors, and perhaps even a demoralized staff of medical professionals, I look to be remembered. I won't be there for my youngest daughter's high school graduation, my oldest daughter's college graduation, either of their wedding days, moments of career success, grandchildren and so on. I'll be gone. I'd love to say "I will miss it," but my brain will be dead and incapable of anything remotely like that. It's not like I'm going to be on some fluffy cloud watching from above with old family members who preceded me, wearing togas, playing the harp, and saying "Congrats Lydia" or "Good Job Izzy!" I wish that were true. Maybe my girls will read this or find my secret letters to them and know it. But, I'll still be gone.

What we long for universally in this death process is to be remembered. I want Lydia and Izzy to remember that I love them. I want my students to remember what I inspired them to do, I want my wife and family to remember me as a "good" man (all the good and valuable things I did, while ignoring my failures and follies). In the end, I just want to be remembered.

If we were all to characterize the things we *want* to be remembered for they will be, I think across the board for most people, for the "good" things. I doubt any reader of this is going to say to themselves, "No, I want to be remembered for hitting my wife, abusing my children, neglecting my work, committing those crimes, and all the work of the Devil I ever did." No one. No one will say that. Instead, it'll circle around to the "goodness."

So, I offer up this: memory is what we live for. We want to be remembered as something more than the embodiment of specific chemicals on this earth for a specific period. We want to be remembered for having embodied value and goodness. If memory *is life* then we need to do several things: we need to improve our memory *and* we need to do good things with our lives. "Goodness" is not derived from our material possessions. We've heard the phrase a thousand times "money can't buy happiness." And it's true. We think it may be true because we get duped. We are bombarded with advertisements and other forms. We know that the food and cave brought us comfort and happiness as proto-humans. So, naturally, more food and a larger cave must translate into more happiness. This, of course, is a myth. It does not. Memory is what we live for and memory is learning. So, we live to learn. And, what I have learned is that life is good.

Real "goodness" comes in giving. The old adage remains in our society because it *is* true: it *is* better to give than to receive. Our greatest (but perhaps least followed) role models were all givers, generous of their time and wisdom and material goods: Buddha, Jesus, Mohammed, Sister Theresa, Gandhi and so on. They gave and they sacrificed. So, if you want to be remembered, you'll need to do some remembering and do some "goodness."

But now, here's the downer. We *are* forgotten. I hate to tell you, but it's true. Time slips on and even despite our best efforts, we forget. I have eleven months to live from the moment I write these words (and hopefully longer), but in eleven months from now, my family and friends will gather and they will collectively remember the life I was blessed to live. A year after that, the stories (and thereby the memories) will decrease. My children will tell stories to their future children (my grandchildren), but their children (my great grandchildren) will know even less. We might have some old mementos, plaques, and pictures, but they too will slowly disappear. Soon,

I will fully join the ranks of my forgotten ancestors: Francis, Francis, Robert, Asa, Orin, Rawson, Silas, Willard and Charles. Soon, my name will end that list. I know their names, but I'm a historian. Yet, I know nothing of the people. I do not know if they were "good men" or not. I know Rawson died during the Civil War fighting for the North. I know Silas was abandoned by his wife and forced to raise three small boys on his own. I know my grandfather Willard committed suicide. But, I do not know them. And so, we forget. And, that obscurity is scary. But it also offers some comfort in that I'm not the first one to be forgotten. We all made our sacrifices by being on this planet and we move on, back into the soil, back into the air, giving back in one last primeval way.

CHAPTER THREE

The Convergence: Memory, History, and The Human Brain

<u>The Reason</u>

The reason memory is critical is pretty obvious. It is reality. I have already noted, at various stages in this work, the reason. Memory was critical to human survival. Being is remembering. "Good or bad," Michael Malone wrote, "memories provide us not only with identity, but existence itself—and to forget, or to be forgotten, is its own kind of death."[71]

Our Proto-Past

I have outlined already, but will do so again, the importance of it in our proto-human past and I will now recount that using the hypothetical character of Grog. Grog is a proto-human. He spends much of his day crouched on the lower

---

[71] Michael Malone, *The Guardian of All Things: The Epic Story of Human Memory.* New York: St. Martin's Press, 2012, xi.

limbs of trees on the African savannah. He occasionally jumps down to eat a passing bug and "remembers" which ones taste good, which ones are full of salty green ooze, and which ones are hard and crunchy. He has his preferences, all based on his "memory" of the bugs he has previously eaten. At another point, Grog sees a passing lion. He "remembers" a previous incident where was almost eaten by a lion that looked much the same. He respectfully keeps his distance and may have even climbed up a few more limbs higher into the tree to avoid being seen. Yet, he also remembers that those same bog cats also often leave their half-eaten prey. He "remembers" the juiciness of the meat, the ease (but risk) by which he got that food. Grog drops to the ground, with one hand still on the tree, he surveys the savannah before him. There are no other predators within sight. He "remembers" hyenas and he "remembers" the pack of other lions, but he doesn't see them. He "remembers" the speed by which he had to gallop to the kill site and off he goes. Memory was central to his survival, our survival.[72]

---

[72] Bloom, 99.

Our Ancient Past

Memory and memorization was also critical in

preliterate cultures.[73] Grog, having evolved into Groggza, son of

Grogz, wanders across central Eurasia, hunting and gathering

with his motley band of like-minded hunters and gatherers.

Groggza, because of his strong memory, leads the group. He

"remembers" the last spring when they stumbled across a grove

of almond trees and a nearby patch of berries. Using his

"memory" of the terrain and his "memory" of the star patterns

that corresponded with that spring harvest, he circles his band

back to the same area. Happily, his people gorge themselves

upon the nuts and berries and hunt the little game found there.

He teaches young band members, using his "memory" of what

his father had taught him, how to make and string a bow. He

teaches them the art of hunting and, as he does, he recounts for

them "from memory" the story of his first mastodon. Groggza's

---

[73] Doidge, 212.

people are happy and Groggza recognized, through "memory", that there were new plants at the site that had been at previous sites they had travelled. He wonders to himself and tries to piece together the story. Did he accidentally bring seeds to this new site? Had his fallen seeds taken root there where they were not native? If so, could he "plant" more there and return to an even greater harvest the following year? Preliterate societies--hunters and gatherers—relied upon their memories of food caches and resource banks to survive. Likewise, they used that memory and their ability to make cause-and-effect connections between their remembered past and the present to initiate agriculture. Then, as Groggza and his descendants became even more gifted at remembering the cycles of the sun and stars and which plants survived and which ones did not, they also recognized which grains could be stored, which ones could be rationed out in hard times, and increasingly they stayed closer and closer to their reliable foodstuffs. Memory made civilization.

Our Civilized Past

Gregory, the descendant of Grog and Groggza, was an ancient scribe. His people living in the fertile valleys between the Tigris and Euphrates, had become so successful at agriculture that they stored vast warehouses of food to feed themselves when life was hard. Their wealth and agricultural prowess was so well known that other bands of roaming savages often spilled into their valley seeking their food. It was becoming more dangerous and more challenging to "remember" the storehouses of food and who did and did not contribute to the community's wealth. The invention of writing, cuneiform, will help resolve that. Man's memory, albeit incredibly powerful, has certain limits. Writing allowed Gregory to use his "memory" of what each character and symbol meant without having to "remember" it all. Writing is, afterall, a mnemonic or memory device. Then, Gregory realized that his work as a scribe was valuable for more than just the business of food storage and the commandments of the King. He realized that the old shaman's stories, now increasingly difficult to share with the growing masses of people in their agricultural society, could be written down and shared. Note here that memory is simply recalled knowledge and that the development of writing was the first step in the democratization of knowledge. What had once been the privileged "memory" of the shaman-poet was now accessible to all those who could learn and remember the new script. All subsequent developments associated with writing have simply been a refinement of that "memory tool." Even our modern computers are just advanced memory tools that allow us to store memories (ergo the use of the term "memory" with regard to computer capacities) and access those memories with greater speed.

Classical Memory

Classical thinkers had their own concepts of what memory was and what it meant. By the age of the renaissance, two competing classical schools of thought about memory dominated: Aristotelian and Platonian. Aristotelian thought suggested memory was instrumental. It served a function.

Platonian concepts of memory, however, saw it as an expression of a "transcendental reality."[74] In short, it was believed that if you could develop and master a mnemonic system (or memory tool set), you might gain insight into the world beyond the everyday existence. It was as if they believed that through memory the heavens might open and all would be known and revealed. By the 16th century, Platonian thinker Giordano Bruno saw "himself as the architect of a synthetic paradigm of the universe that would provide its practitioners with insight into a deep structural reality of all knowledge of heaven and earth."[75] Giambattista Vico, a teacher of rhetoric, believed that through mnemonic skills and text analysis the poetic knowledge of the universe would be exposed and the practitioner would gain access to the collective memory of that universe. By the end of the 17th century, this mystical memory tour would end. The onset of inductive science under Bacon and others would shift ideas about memory away.[76]

---

[74] Hutton, 30-31.
[75] Hutton, 31.
[76] Hutton, 37; Daniel Gordon, Book Review of "History as an Art of

Memory and the Scientific Age

Beginning in the 17th century and then flourishing over 18th and 19th centuries, thinkers began examining "memory" from a scientific perspective. For example, in 1882 Ribot in his work *Diseases of Memory* wrote about the fundamental properties of memory, including "registration and recollection." This was an early delineation between the process of imprinting (or registering) a memory in the mind and the process of retrieving (or recollecting) that memory. Ribot recognized that they were two distinct, but interrelated processes.[77] Ribot's contemporary, William James in his 1890 classic work *Principles of Psychology* further noted the difference between primary memory (short-term memory) and secondary memory (long-term memory).[78]

Memory," by Patrick Hutton, *History and Theory,* v34, n4, December 1996: 341-342.

[77] Mark R. Rosenzweig, "The Psychological Approach to Human Memory," in Mark R. Rosenzweig and Edward L. Bennett, eds. *Neural Mechanisms of Learning and Memory.* Cambridge: M.I.T. Press, 1976, 3.

[78] Rosenzweig, 3-4.

Today, we have made significant strides in our understanding of the complex workings of the brain and memory, but we still have much to do. What we have learned in the last 100 years, however, is significant. We have slowly moved away from the card-catalog analogy that allowed us to envision memory as a giant library card-catalog file whereby an individual recorded discreet memories on tiny slips of paper that were organized in some fashion in a complex, poorly cross-referenced system. Now, we know that this analogy has abundant flaws. As Kandel has noted, "the cellular mechanisms of learning and memory reside not in the special properties of the neuron itself, but in the connections it receives and makes with other cells in the neuronal circuit to which it belongs."[79] Memory is not a single place or a single discreet unit, but a process. It is a fluid, dynamic, organic and interactive phenomenon. Moreover, as many have noted, human minds vary in such significant ways that memory is also, to a significant degree, idiosyncratic to the individual.[80]

---

[79] Kandel, 142.

The fluid and dynamic nature of memory is made possible, in part, by the complex structure of the brain cells. Some nerve cells, for example, have as many as 50 dendritic branches reaching off them. In doing so, they allow for a whole variety of complex connections to be made.[81] Think of it this way, if dendritic branches (part of the transmission structure within the brain's synaptic exchange) were like friends and each friend connected to another series of friends in the same manner, then our friendship patterns would grow exponentially. In the brain, these dendritic branches allow us to make millions of connections and, as a result, millions of images and memories (both small and large, short and long-term). It really is a vast complex, frontier.

The communication between cells is equally complicated. One nerve cell (faster than you can say Jack Robinson) can communicate with a second nerve cell by releasing a neurotransmitter, or a chemical signal.[82] "The

---

[80] Kandel, 65-69.
[81] Kandel, 65.
[82] Kandel, 60-65.

second cell recognizes the signal and responds by means of a specific molecule on its surface membrane called a receptor."[83] This is important for scientists to understand, but for us liberal arts folks it has a secondary value. We need to recognize that the brain is, for all intents and purposes, an electro-chemical machine. So what? Well, we need to understand that the chemical make-up of our brain is ever-changing. Some studies suggest that a child's brain formation is not entirely complete until the late 20s. No wonder we did such stupid stuff in college, huh? Moreover, because it is a chemical apparatus, it is subject to chemical changes. Diet, alcohol or drug use, depression and other emotions (good and bad) can influence our brain functioning.

So, the process of memory formation and consolidation occurs across the brain and at various times and stages. Short-term memories, for example, are converted to long-term memories in the hippocampus and then stored back in the original areas of perception.[84] Unconscious memories, as

---

[83] Kandel, 60.

Milner has demonstrated, reside "outside the hippocampus and the medial temporal lobe."[85]   Moreover, as LeDoux in *The Emotional Brain* has noted, "sensory signals go directly to the amygdala, bypassing the sensory cortex before we are even aware of them. This so-called 'lower' route begins to make meaning of our experience before we have begun to understand it."[86] In short, we are beginning the process of all "thinking" and "memory storage" before we have even recognized that we are doing it.

Once inside, memories are constantly being refashioned.[87] This is what some scholars have referred to as the "plasticity" of the mind.[88]   Indeed, even before the neuroscience breakthroughs of the late 20th century, there were those who understood that principle. Sigmund Freud himself referred to the "plastic view of memory."[89] In short, we know that because of the many connections and potential circuits

---

[84] Kandel, 130.
[85] Kandel, 129.
[86] Zull, 59.
[87] Doidge, 229.
[88] Pinker, 215.
[89] Doidge, 224.

that memories can follow, that memories will change. It's like the course of a river. Over time, changes in the environment and climate may affect that river's route. So too with memory. New memories, new information, and new connections can affect the nature of a memory and, in doing so, its interpretation. This is not only its "plasticity" but its interactive, ever-changing dynamic nature.[90]

Implicit memories like those involving specific skills and habits or those behaviors to which we have been conditioned are stored in the cerebellum, striatum, and amygdala.[91] But, not all memories are stored in the same places. For the sake of this discussion, however, it is worth noting that the storage of "episodic memories" are often close to one another.[92] So, because it's not unusual for the memory of friends or characters from movies to be housed in close proximity to one another, it

---

[90] Philosopher Michel Foucault has argued there is a "plasticity of human nature" and a "discontinuous nature of history." It only makes sense that if the brain and memory have "plasticity" and history is memory and history is human nature, that human nature has this same "plasticity." Gordon, 341; Hutton, 109.

[91] Kandel, 130.

[92] Hofstadter, 85.

is perhaps not surprising that we access these "characters" from our memory in our dreams. Why else might my dream have my friend Walt Bithell in the same room with Charles Manson, Ed McMahon, and Socrates? These episodic memories appear to be most strongly associated with the right frontal cortex whereas semantic memories (those involving labels, facts, and names) are more closely connected to the left frontal cortex.[93] Now, this is where memory has become critical to the ways in which we teach. If we want students to remember the totality of what we are instructing them on, we need to catalyze both their semantic and episodic memories and stimulate the connections between the left and right frontal cortices.

Clearly, there are a whole host of reasons *why* we have memory. First and foremost, it has allowed us as a species to survive. The first little proto-human that jumped from the tree, crawled to another spindly tree on the border of the savannah, and looked out onto to that vast grassland had to have had a

---

[93] Zull, 79-80.

memory of some sort. As she pulled herself up by one arm to get a better glimpse of that sea of danger, she had better have a good memory about where she came from—because larger, meaner, proto-human-eating predators were out there waiting for her. They slobbered all over themselves in anticipation of that tasty little proto-human. But, when the time came and they decided to pounce, they discovered that the little helpless creature had safely retreated to her old tree. And so it has gone for millennia. We remembered the safety of our trees. We remembered where we had cached nuts and where wild huckleberries grew in abundance. We remembered the stars and, in doing so, we remembered when to plant our crops and harvest them. Memory has, in short, been central to the survival and evolution of the human species. Again, Bloom said "memory is the core of what we call reality."[94] But, we now know that that "reality" has been, in part, fabricated in our heads. Our brian, in short, processes "semifictional realities of our own life story."[95]

---

[94] Bloom, 72.

It may seem less important today with all of our modern technology, but our memory is still critical. And, I believe as a historian, it's just as important today to know where we came from as it was for that little proto-human thousands upon thousands of years ago. It marks out for us the path to safety and security. It defines for us our course toward success. It doesn't mean that we cannot change. It does not mean that we have to stay so close to the tree that we can never venture out further onto the savannah and embrace new experiences. What it does mean, perhaps, is that we ought to consistently remember that we are human—frail, vulnerable, and weak. It is that humility, drawn from the lessons of memory, that may serve as a critical key to our future survival. In short, as a weak species (lacking substantive size, speed, or large sharp teeth), memory was central to our survival. We needed to remember where the watering holes were, where the best nuts and berries could be foraged, who we could trust and cooperate with, and

---

[95] Austin, 71.

how to plant, harvest, follow the stars and so forth. Memory was the human advantage.

Memory also serves to guide us in other ways. Guilt, for example, is a form of memory. As a Catholic, I know guilt. I think Guilt may have actually roomed with me in college. It's as central to Catholic as papal infallibility, cheering for Notre Dame, and the feast of Seven Fishes. It's just what we do. Today, some folks look down upon guilt and I can see their point to a degree. But, the fact remains that guilt (in its healthy forms) can serve as a guide for appropriate moral behavior. If I were to take your plate of cookies and eat them without your consent, knowledge, and approval, I really ought to feel guilty about it. As tasty as they were, I should know that committing that crime against you—whether it's a misdemeanor or felony— is not good. That knowledge of appropriate behavior that creeps into our minds *after* we have done something wrong is a strong memory and we call it "guilt." It's a memory. We remembered the rules after having done something wrong. Hopefully, that memory (aka guilt) will remind us NOT to do that again. Hopefully, the feeling of guilt will compel us to act more appropriately. But, again, it's a memory. Likewise, memories of others can also compel us. My father wasn't the greatest father, but his misdeeds have compelled me to be *Great* father. As comedian Jim Gaffigan, author of *Dad is Fat*, wrote: "My father may not have been the best dad, but without comparisons to him, I would probably feel guiltier, so in a way he made me a better dad."[96] Memory serves us in the personal realm just as HISTORY ought to serve us in the public realm. Why can't we judge President George W. Bush and say, "I may want to have a beer with the guy and he seems nice enough, but he was a really really crappy president."? Our survival as a species (and I'd argue as a planet) hinges on our ability to make thoughtful and insightful observations, make generalizations based upon specific substantive evidence, and then act accordingly. I will NOT vote for a president like George Bush again. My memory is too strong to make that mistake.

---

[96] Jim Gaffigan, *Dad is Fat*. New York: Crown Archetype, 2013, 38.

Guilt is just one form of memory. Frankly, all of our decisions—every single one from the act of putting our feet on the ground every morning to more complex decisions within our profession—hinges upon memory and is filtered through our memory. Thinking is just an act of memory. I dare you, for example, to conjure up a thought *not* using memory. It can't be done. The task assigned to you is already rooted in the past and is, therefore, a decision involving memory.

Historians as Guardians of Memory

If memories are an individual's recollection of the past, then perhaps what historians do is to preserve memories of the past. Perhaps, we are guardians of the past, guardians of memory.[97] And, the implications are clear: if we do away with historians we run the risk of losing those memories and that past becomes lost to us and we become warped in our

---

[97] Herodotus is often credited with the concept of historians as "guardians of memory." See Olick, 192. Yerushalmi has even gone so far as to say that "For Herodotus the writing of history was first and foremost a bulwark against the inexorable erosion of memory engendered by the passage of time." See Olick, 201.

understanding of ourselves. Paul Edwards, author of *To Acknowledge A War: The Korean War in American Memory* (2000) wrote, "When nations, like individuals, try to rewrite the past in such a way as to ignore its impact, they are likely to become sick, and their affirmations to become obsessions."[98] Those obsessions then run the risk of evolving into national myths and serve as a greater stumbling block to a clear and accurate history of that particular people.[99]

It's not that history cannot be interpreted in a variety of ways. There are, after all, a whole host of different perspectives and experiences. To disallow any change in interpretation is an even greater tragedy. "In frozen memory," Huyssen writes, "the past is nothing but the past."[100] It behooves us all then to figure out the relationship between memory and history and how that relationship will unfold over time. This is an "interesting theoretical challenge."[101] What makes it so interesting and

---

[98] Edwards, 18 in Wulf Kansteiner, "Finding Meaning in Memory: A Methodological Critique of Collective Memory Studies," *History and Theory* 41 (May 2002), 186, fn31.

[99] Andreas Huyssen, *Twilight Memories: Marking Time in a Culture of Amnesia*. New York: Routledge, 2012, 250.

[100] Huyssen, 260.

challenging is that the whole process is organic, dynamic, and interactive. History is the collective memory of a certain past, but when recorded it adds itself to the memory and re-makes a new history. Roland Barthes argues that all authors take existing texts and then offer them back in new ways. That author and then every subsequent reader imbues the new text with new meanings. And so it is for history. Gadamer refers to this as a "fusion of horizons" whereby historians recognize that their understanding of the past stems, in large part, from their own immersion in cultural traditions and forces from that very past.[102] As guardians of memory, historians (and all those who participate in historical recollection) are like "imaginary relay teams."[103] On the individual side, we take the memories passed down to us from our parents and grandparents and we hand them off to our children and grandchildren. Memories, like relay batons , make their journeys down through generations of descendants. Likewise, historians do the same and we openly

---

[101] Kansteiner, 184.
[102] Hutton, 23.
[103] Zerubavel, 58.

acknowledge the Academic Family Tree. I was a student of Robert Swartout, who was a student of Gordon Dodds, who was a student of Frederick Merk, who was a student of Frederick Jackson Turner, and so on and so on. We are proud of our lineage and we are proud of the noble objective we try to pursue—preserve the memory, preserve the history.

New interpretations, new meanings, and new histories, however, does not mean all out fabrications of the past. Under ideal circumstances, but not always, historians "purify arguments" and, in the process, limit the possible spectrum of lies, mistruths, and fabrications.[104] Interestingly enough, it is the difference in those interpretations that drives a student's inquiry into the past. In effect, they were told one thing by Mrs. McGillicuddy, a second interpretation by Mr. Potratz, and a third by Coach Schmucker and when those students get to college and sit in my classroom, they are amazed at the

---

[104] Jan-Werner Muller, "Introduction: The Power of Memory, the Memory of Power, and the Power Over Memory," in Jan-Werner Muller, ed., *Memory and Power in Post-War Europe: Studies in the Presence of the Past* Cambridge: Cambridge University Press, 2002, 23.

discordance between the various interpretations and have the opportunity to play it out in their own heads, form their own conclusions, and add to that myriad of accounts.[105]

Now, some folks (particularly those on the Far Right) will suggest that I am unpatriotic and that my interpretation of the past was not only a negative portrayal of our nation, but inaccurate. Of course, I have facts behind all my lectures, but my presentations certainly do not idealize the past or our nation's role in world affairs. They do, however, try to make sense of who we are and who we want to be. As a historian, therefore, I am not only a guardian of the past and an analyst of that past, but I am also an analyst of our recollections of that past.[106] Now, my right-wing critics may have a point. It does seem that there is a pervasive "liberal" element in academic institutions, particularly in the discipline of history, but it has less to do with certain power levels in American society than it does with other factors at play. First, students who pursue

---

[105] Gordon, 350-351.
[106] Malone, 270.

history generally do not come from conservative backgrounds. Those students are typically encouraged to get a degree in business or engineering are typically pushed in certain directions in education where the degree translates to a clearly defined vocation or career. History students may have career plans, but they are as numerous as the stars. Many of our students pursue history because they love the subject and want to explore. Secondly, there is a certain "mind-opening" process by studying history. One learns that the world is much more complex than the binary black-and-white way it has been portrayed in the media and that by understanding the follies and foibles of the human past and the human tragedies associated with that past that one becomes more empathetic to the human experience of the present. There are a whole host of other reasons that compel historians toward liberalism. And let's admit, not all of us are liberals.

There are conservatives and arch-conservatives lurking among us. But, it is the vast gap in interpretations between academic historians and right-wing politics that makes for interesting (and often frustrating news). The Texas School Board's decision, without the consultation of any significant body of historians, to rewrite the Texas history textbooks and eliminate huge portions relevant to Native American history and Latino history was born out of political bias and motive, not out of academic integrity.

This is not new. Much of the United States' 19th century written history was pure fabrication. It was myth. We elevated our Founding Fathers into mythic heroes who could throw stones across the Potomac, never told lies, and so forth. Portraits of our leaders were painted in togas with classical Greek and Roman backgrounds. We lied to ourselves to make ourselves feel better. We wanted to believe that we had overthrown tyranny in favor of classical Athenian democracy. Yet, the truth remained that we separated ourselves from Britain (the greatest bastion of freedom to that date and birthplace of Parliament and representative government) and replaced it with Virginian slave-owning aristocracy. So, we fudged the truth a little to make ourselves feel better about that "false revolution." Then, to make sure we had sufficiently distanced ourselves from those pesky Brits, we latched onto a heroic figure who was NOT British at all....enter Christopher Columbus.

The United States is not the only nation who have wrestled with and redefined their national past. The French Revolution of 1830, it has been argued, was a product of revolutionary memory from 1789. The Russians tried to rewrite their past (and purge it, pun intended) after their Revolution in 1919. Germany, Israel, Japan, and many of the eastern European nations have reexamined their past in the wake of WWII. It is, I would argue, part of the process of memory and history.[107]

The question becomes, as has been asked by Muller, "Is there a categorical imperative to remember? And is remembrance possible, or even desirable, without retribution, restoration, or restitution?"[108] It has become increasingly clear

---

[107] Hutton, 131-133.
[108] Muller, 31.

that "not remembering" or "forgetting" is a critical human function. It not only allows us to prioritize thoughts, but also make space for new, more important memories. So, we imprint just about every sensation we experience (some without knowing it) and we then proceed to unwittingly forget many of those memories because they are not actively serving us in any significant way. Those memories that do remain have been stored, warped by other thoughts, and recalled in new and more various ways. "To function at all, "Jacqueline Dowd Hall writes, "we must forget most of the scenes and sensations that constitute the vast rush of 'experience' or overlay them with what Sigmund Freud called 'screen memories,' memories that protect us from fear, anxiety, and pain."[109]

---

[109] Jacqueline Dowd Hall, "'You Must Remember This': Autobiography as Social Critique," in Nancy Bercaw, ed. *Gender and the Southern Body Politic*. Jackson: University Press of Mississippi, 2000, 1-2.

CHAPTER FOUR

United We Think, Divided We Fall: Collective Memory

We know we have individual memories and we also know that we have a collective past. In between those two lay a critical and important middle-ground: collective memory. For many groups, group memory or collective memory is critical for identity and identity preservation. For Jews, for example, their history as a people had been dependent upon the story of their exile and exodus. Their story has taken on new significance with the added historical burden of having survived (and lost so many in) the Holocaust. But for other groups, their past collective experiences have also been formative. It may be the institution of slavery for African-Americans, 9/11 for New Yorkers, the Confederate flag for southern whites and so on.[110] The collective memory within which they have been acculturated shapes not only their understanding of that past,

---

[110] Zerubavel, 3.

their value of the symbols associated with that past, but how

they respond to current issues revolving around those same

issues. It is not surprising then that we have a cultural war over

the Confederate flag. It is, after all, a contest of cultural

memory: those who see the flag as emblematic of their

rebellious heritage and that of their grandparents versus those

who see it as representative of the society that once enslaved

them.[111]

Collective Memory: Who Remembers What?

The collective memory of the past is shaped, in large

part, by the collective consciousness of a people. The term,

"collective consciousness," was coined by sociologist Emile

---

[111] The idea of "collective memory" and its relationship to history has only been an American intellectual endeavor since the 1980s. The French have long been wrestling with this and have made huge contributions to the larger theoretical issues at play. They have also done many important works on the subject as it relates to French history. My thanks to Prof. Charles LeGuin at Portland State University for first introducing me to the subject when I was a master's student there.

Durkheim in the 19ᵗʰ century as a term referring to a set of shared values, beliefs, and moral attitudes. As Jacqueline Dowd Hall wrote, "In all these ways, we live both the history we have learned through reading and research and the history we have experienced and inherited, passed down through the groups with which we identify, sedimented in the body, and created through talk."[112] The first explicit use of the term "collective memory" came in 1902 by Hugo von Hofmannsthal when he described it as a "dammed up force of our mysterious ancestors within us."[113] One of Durkheim's pupils, Maurice Halbwachs, took the idea one step further. Halbwachs argued that memory was dependent upon a framework within which a group was positioned in society.[114] He suggested that while history emphasized differences between the past and present, memory emphasized the similarities.[115] As a result, he regarded memory

---

[112] Dowd Hall, 3.

[113] Jeffrey Olick and Joyce Robbins, "Social Memory Studies: From 'Collective Memory' to the Historical Sociology of Mnemonic Practices," *American Review of Sociology,* 24, (1998), 106.

[114] Halbwachs was also a socialist. Arrested by the Gestapo in Nazi Germany after protesting his Jewish father-in-law's arrest, he was ultimately sent to Buchenwald where he died in Macrh 1945.

[115] Hutton, 76.

as "protean and elusive" while history was "durable and verifiable."[116] For Halbwachs, collective memory sat juxtaposed to individual memory, two separate but similarly structured phenomena.[117] But let's see the two (the group and the individual) phenomena as correlated rather than interrelated. In fact, there are those who suggest that the relationship between the two (at least in some societies) has an inverse correlation. Hutton, for example, has written, "The exteriorization of collective memory in public institutions designed to store them is complemented by the deepening interiorization of individual memory."[118] The more our individual memories become "just ours", individualized, and isolated from modern society, the more likely we are to see a growth in the exteriorized public memories of our larger groups. In short, awash in the swarm of modern life, swimming to maintain our own unique identities, we often clutch to public

---

[116] Hutton, 76.

[117] Kansteiner, 184. On Halbwachs' sharp division between individual and collective memories, Kansteiner stated "the idea of an individual memory, absolute separate from social memory, is an abstraction almost devoid of meaning."

[118] Hutton, 151.

expressions of identity as if it were a buoy or life-preserver in the undercurrent of a vast ocean. Fragmentation in society compels us to seek new, fabricated and imagined connections.[119]

Case Study in Collective Memory: The Confederate Flag

But, as suggested earlier, these "collective memories" are rarely written or expressed by one individual (except when artificially created for some regime or another). Instead, "collective memory" has a certain level of consensus.[120] They are forged through shared experiences (like rallies and marches) and articulated in conversations with one another, through reunions, social media, old photographs, cultural organizations, and re-enactments.[121] Collectively, these groups maintain THEIR version of the past and, in doing so, make it their own reality.[122] Now, this is pretty evident to us in 2015 when we reflect upon that cultural war over the Confederate flag. Two of

---

[119] Gordon, 350.

[120] Iwona Irwin-Zarecka, *Frames of Remembrance: The Dynamics of Collective Memory.* New Brunswick, NJ: Transaction Publishers, 2007, 67.

[121] Irwin-Zarecka, 55.

[122] Irwin-Zarecka, 54.

the main contestants in that struggle are the NAACP and the

Sons of the Confederacy. The first (the National Association for

the Advancement of Colored Persons) is an African-American

civil rights organization born in the early 20th century as a

response to the unfulfilled promises of the 13th, 14th, and 15th

amendments and the failure of the first American civil rights

movement known as Reconstruction. The latter is an

organization of largely white descendants of men who served in

the Confederacy and sought to preserve the value of the "Old

South" on the heels of their resounding defeat and their

bitterness afterwards. Both groups have their own "collective

memory" and, in doing so, have interpreted the past in ways

suitable to their values and needs. But, as Halbwachs noted,

"memory is only able to endure within sustaining social

contexts. Individual images of the past are provisional. They

are 'remembered' only when they are located within the

conceptual structures that are defined by communities at

large."[123] So, the struggle we have been witness to between

---

[123] Hutton, 6.

African-Americans and their civil rights allies and the Confederate flag-waving traitors of the South is a product of changing social values whereby African-Americans were given a voice and, finally, an opportunity to express their history, their historical interpretations, and play their share in the construction of those "collective memories." Had they not been given their freedom or been forced to continue their pitiful existence under Jim Crow and segregation, there would be no debate or struggle as the white Confederate version of that past (the one that dominated from 1865 to 1965) would still be preeminent. Yet, the great irony in this story is that had not the Confederate flag supporters so vehemently resisted, the individual memories of the 1950s and 1960s and its civil rights movements would have withered away and the flag would simply be an odd, unknown relic to a distant past. The cases of police brutality and racial profiling throughout the nation in the last few years, coupled with the trench warfare-like mentality of the KKK and other flag supporters, has reinvented and reinvigorated their counter groups' cultural identity.[124]

Where is Our History? Who Owns and Who Can Afford it?

This phenomenon of forming and forging a "collective memory" does not only occur within particular social groups, racial and ethnic groups, or national identities, but also within and between generations. Individuals who were born before the Great Depression and who survived it as young people, for example, are a community in time. These "age cohorts" have a set of experiences that allow them to establish values and beliefs based on that "shared past."[125] When a set of individuals share an unique body of experiences, they often believe that no one else could possibly understand what it was like. My mother, for example, would say that kids today had no idea what it was like living through the abject poverty of the 1930s or what sacrifices were made to survive that era. It affected my mother's understanding of the Great Depression, but it also

---

[124] See Hutton, 6 regarding group confirmation and individual memories.
[125] Irwin-Zarecka, 53.

influenced her attitude about money, savings, and material wealth. Moreover, it shaped her attitudes toward others. It defined her and, in doing so, distinguished her. It was, after all, her identity.

The civil rights movement and other "identity" movements in American history (today and in the past) are to a certain degree an effort to redress the past. Abuses and oppression took its toll on a whole host of peoples—from American Indians to the descendants of former slaves, from those hunted and purged from our government during the Lavender Scare to the Japanese-Americans interned in camps during World War Two.. It is natural that they seek redress now that their position in society has been affected, albeit not entirely fixed. They have sought to regain their memory of their collective past, restore their position in recorded history, and gain social recognition of that change and that past abuse. In doing so, "memory is marshalled as grievance and as a claim on political resources."[126]

---

[126] Muller, 17.

Historian Michael Kammen has suggested that the post-1980s infatuation with "memory" stems, in large part, from America's embrace of multiculturalism. In short, as we became more tolerant and accepting of others, those "others" sought to better remember their past, follow the traces of their collective memory, and install it into the American memory landscape.[127]

The concept of "collective memory" is often used interchangeably (rightly and wrongly) with terms like "social memory," "collective remembrance," "popular history-making," "national memory," "vernacular memory," and "counter memory."[128] What distinguishes all of them from "individual memory," however, is that they are collectively constructed and housed in a society's "inventory of signs and symbols"—like monuments, memorials, and commemorative traditions.[129] Individual memories are expressed in a much more subtle and interior way. Individual memories are, for all intents and

---

[127] Kammen (1995) in Olick and Robbins, 107.
[128] Kansteiner, 181.
[129] Kansteiner, 188.

purposes, warehoused in the brain and occasionally in personal journals and memoirs. Rarely do individual memories see the light of day. Collective memories, in contrast, are almost always expressed in a variety of ways and rarely do not have some public form of expression. These collective public memories can be seen in public holidays, museums, memorials, building inscriptions, and even public commercial advertisements. Certain marketing agencies' use of the images of Lincoln or Washington or Franklin are capitalizing on the idea of American-ness for those particular products much in the same way that a sexy woman stretched across the hood of a car sells that product. Lincoln and Washington may not be sexy and, thereby, titillating, but they do inform the consumer that it's an All-American good--wise, traditional, and worthy of your patronage.[130] They play into the American exceptionalism we've been sold by our grade school teachers. Zerubavel might refer to this as "iconic connectedness" whereby there are

---

[130] Theodor Adorno and Max Horkheimer coined the term "culture industry" to refer to the many ways in which entrepreneurs have engaged in the capitalist mass production of cultural standards.

deliberate efforts to link something new to an older historic item for the sake of playing on that connection and its value in the community. Look in any phonebook and check out business names. In Erie, Pennsylvania, you'll find a number of businesses with the name "Niagara" in them, not because we are so close to the great waterfall. It's almost 2 hours away. During the war of 1812, Oliver Hazard Perry quickly constructed a small fleet on the Erie waterfront to help repel the British from the Great Lakes. When he successfully accomplished that, his ship, the *Brig Niagara* became a local (if not national) legend. Local businesses are still playing on that icon over 100 years later. Further west up the Lake Erie shoreline is Cleveland, Ohio which, among many many wonderful things, is also home to the Great Lakes Brewery. That brewery features several historically-named beers, but my favorite is their "Burning River." This beer was named after a tragic event in the city's not-so-distant past. In 1969, because of horrible pollution being dumped in the city's Cuyahoga River, the river caught fire. It became a symbol of the Rustbelt and a symbol of the city's failures and decline. But, the Great Lake Brewing Company has embraced its past and named a beer for that horrible event. In doing so, it has taken much of the fire out of that tragedy's sting and serves as a new testament to the toughness and sense of humor of the city's entrepreneurs. It's also helps when it's a good beer—which it is (send all complimentary beers to my address listed at the end, ahem.)   "Collective memory," Zerubavel argues, "continuously negotiates between available historical records and current social and political agendas."[131] That continuous negotiation means that the "collective memory" is really just another form of historical interpretation. A society's collective memory," Huyssen notes, "is no less contingent, no less unstable, its shape by no means permanent. It is always subject to subtle and not so subtle reconstruction."[132]

---

[131] Yael Zerubavel, *Recovered Roots: Collective Memory and the Making of Israeli National Tradition.* Chicago: University of Chicago Press, 1995, 5.
[132] Huyssen, 249.

At this point, you ought to have a reasonably basic understanding of "collective memory." But, let's make it absolutely clear here how important this "collective memory" is to a society. Memory, and all its manifestations within a particular society, constitute that society's "culture."[133]

A Place in Time

Culture and "collective memory" are expressed in a variety of ways. Individuals make pilgrimages to certain places to celebrate a specific past and reinvigorate their memory of that historical tradition. These pilgrimages, by the way, are not always religious in nature. In fact, as Americans we engage in a whole host of historical pilgrimages. We visit national parks like Yellowstone to reinvigorate our "collective memory" of our own youth, the rugged American frontier, and so on. We visit Cooperstown and Canton, very unique mnemonic communities, so we can become closer to those American past-times of

---

[133] Halil Turan, "Memory and the Myth of Prometheus," in Anna-Teresa Tymieniecka, *Memory in the Ontopoiesis of Life.* New York: Springer, 2009, 10.

baseball and football.[134] We visit museums, national monuments and memorials, national historic sites, and the like. Millions of Americans visit Washington, D.C., but they do so not to participate in democracy or our representative government, but to tour about the monuments and memorials, classical structures designed to elevate our past, and convince ourselves that we have (despite tons of evidence) the greatest nation on the planet. In doing all of these "collective memory visits," we are allowed to come into closer "contact" with our collective past.[135] Hut has captured this in a much more poetic way. He wrote, "Places of memory are like 'moments of history torn away from the movement of history, then returned. No longer quite alive, not yet dead, they are like seashells on the shore from which the sea of living memory has retreated.'"[136] Indeed, by the 1980s, a body of new scholarship began to emerge focusing exclusively on the history of commemoration.[137]

---

[134] Eviatar Zerubavel, 42.
[135] Eviatar Zerubavel, 42.
[136] Hutton, 152.
[137] Hutton, 2.

Huyssen suggests that modern society's obsession with

"memory" stems from the temporality of the modern world.

We are developing technologies at an exponential pace,

captivated by smaller and smaller and faster and faster bytes of

information. In short, our world is speeding by and Huyssen

suggests that it is for that reason that we have increasingly

grasped onto "memory."[138] But that examination and

scholarship of memory certainly did merit examination. By the

21st century, there were over 1200 institutions and initiatives in

Germany alone dedicated to museums, memorials, or

monuments dedicated to the Holocaust.[139] Some have

suggested, however, that this "inflation" in history and memory

may be problematic in that its expansion (as if it followed a

supply and demand model) might make it less valuable if not

meaningless.[140] It is, as Zerubavel suggests, a response to the

"increasing evanescence of things."[141]

---

[138] Huyssen, 6. Huyssen calls this a "hypertrophy of historical
consciousness."
[139] Gordon, 352
[140] Gordon, 352.
[141] Eviatar Zerubavel, 41.

Memorials and monuments are one thing, but museums are an altogether different beast. Monuments and memorials serve as reminders to a past through a new structure—whether it be an obelisk like the Washington Monument or a series of statues like the Korean War Memorial in Washington, D.C. Those structures did not exist at the time of the event or individual being commemorated. Museums, in contrast, "house" artifacts from the period under study. It is both a memorialization and a musealisation.[142] "Real" and "historical" objects are extracted from their original or natural environment and placed under glass, on display, in a museum. In doing so, the museum has conferred upon that subject new meaning and purpose.[143] And, as Sch has noted, "every decision to collect and preserve something for purposes other than expressly for its utilitarian function" changes the intent.[144] In

---

[142] Muller, 16.

[143] Chang Wen-Chen, "A Cross-Cultural Perspective on Musealization: The Museum's Reception in China and Japan in the second half of the nineteenth century," *Museum and Society* 10 (1) March 2012, 15.

[144] Martin Scharer, "Things + Ideas+ Musealization= Heritage: A Methodological Approach," Keynote at Academic Year of the Graduate Program in Museology and Heritage, PPG-PMUS, UNIRIO/MAST, Rio de Janeiro, 17 March 2008, 3.

doing so, the objects are converted from "items" to "musealia" and "the object is saved through its 'death.'"[145]

For those who cannot travel, there is another option for engaging in the "collective memory." Millions of Americans collect stamps, football and baseball memorabilia, beer labels, and so forth. They are amateur (and not-so-amateur) antiquarians whereby the mementos they have saved, preserved, and hoarded all help bridge a gap between themselves in the indistinguishable present by embracing the remarkable and distinguishable past.[146] Collectibles also often serve as powerful reminders of our youth. I maintain a series of collections because they remind me of my days back in Boise, Idaho and all the children with whom I was associated. When I see my 1970 Topps Joe Namath card I think of my brother and my stay in the hospital for a hernia surgery. When I see my 1971 Topps Bart Starr card, I not only think how much I hate the Green Bay Packers, but I remember the day when I almost

---

[145] Scharer, 4.
[146] Eviaton Zerubavel, 44.

traded it for seven or eight cards missing from my 1976 complete set. Thank God my brother went with me to enforce a trade-back after I experienced a severe case of "buyer's remorse."

Culture and the ways in which a society expresses its history are important. How that history is expressed is equally vital.[147] The process begins even before the end of the historical event in question. Once the "event" has transpired, contemporary commentators twist the storyline to reinforce their particular agenda or weaken or attack their opponents. While historians make efforts to objectively assess the historical "event," the public's assessment of the "event" is often taking it into altogether different realms. The voices of the public "collective memory" are often loud. At the moment, for example, the critics of the Obama Administration have a platform that accords them a loud and seemingly dominant position in the shaping of "collective memory" about Obama.

---

[147] Eviaton Zerubavel, 2, 13.

But, while they are loud, the historians' writings and long-term assessment has greater wherewithal. It would not surprise me then that in 25 to 50 years, the pendulum will have fully swung. Obama may, in 2065, be regarded as one of the greatest U.S. presidents in modern history. So, to remind ourselves— contemporary forces may be loud and powerful in the short-term shaping of "collective memory," historians (as the guardians of that memory) have a greater long-term force. I am using those terms deliberately as I believe there is a direct parallel between the science of individual memories and the functioning of collective memories. We collect and briefly store certain memories (like contemporary social commentators), but those ideas are often shuttled and forgotten for the more valuable memories. Certain short-term memories are transferred into long-term memory (via the work of historians) where it serves to guide that society and provide its formative cultural identity.

But these collective memories do not abet simply one group or smaller sub-groups, they also serve the individual.

Acquiring a group's memory is critical to social identity and thereby personal identity.[148] You can say what you will about Rachel Dolezal and her fabrication that she was African-American and, in doing so, rose through the ranks of the Spokane chapter of the NAACP. It appears by evidence at this point that she truly felt more akin with the African-American community and felt more in tune with that group's memory than she did her own traditional white background. Now, this may be a perfect example of "white privilege" and I acknowledge that, but without knowing the inner workings of her mind, I'm not sure anyone will truly understand the full story as to why a white woman would adopt the status of an oppressed minority. At any rate, this is all part of group memory and its influence upon personal identity. My family is Welsh and Dutch on my father's side, but we had no cultural markers or group history or memory to guide us and help us retain that "memory." My mother's family were Volgadeutsche, German farmers who had been taken to Russia

---

[148] Eviaton Zerubavel, 3.

in the mid-1700s as a part of Catherine the Great's efforts to improve Russian agriculture. They spoke German, lived German lives, and married within their German communities. But they lived in Russia. When my family came to the U.S. after 1900, they retained many of their cultural traits and passed them down through the generations. I ate Volgadeutsche foods, knew some German words, and knew the story of my family's persecution in Czarist Russia. I was, by virtue of the strength of their collective memory, capable of using that history to help forge my own identity. I believed I understood oppression even though I came from a solidly middle class existence. I understood the hardship of immigration even though the farthest I had ever been forced to move was from Salem, Oregon to Boise, Idaho when I was 6 years old. I have used my appreciation of history and my understanding of my family's "collective memory" to carve out for myself a certain type of empathy and compassion. It has shaped my personal identity. It's also worth noting that it was my experience doing genealogy with my mother at the LDS Genealogy Center in Boise that sparked my life-long interest in history. Philippe Aries, a great historian and thinker, believed that the "memory of one's own heritage...is the most enticing lure into historical inquiry."[149]

"Memory" and "collective memory" also serve as an identity adhesive. Let's face it, we change. Our bodies change. Human cells are constantly re-shaping us and sometimes in increasingly varied ways. When I was 20 years old, I had a full head of curly long blonde hair, piercing blue eyes, an eagle-like nose, and two dimples. By the time I was 40, I had lost most of my hair, what little that remained had darkened significantly, and my eyes were a softer blue but surrounded by a growing body of wrinkles. Only my dimples stayed the same. Now, as I approach 50 years of age, I am yet again different. My hair fell out last year during chemotherapy and has since returned in an all-white state. My goatee is white as well. My eyes may still be piercing, but the color there has shaded into green and my dimples still shoot up the sides of my smiling and laughing face. I look amazingly different than I did when I was 20 or 10 or 2

---

[149] Hutton, 91.

years old. What has persisted, however, is my memory. I have

maintained a "memory of self" such that I have appeared to be

"stable" in my condition and I am able to be the "same person."[150]

This transferal of memory, from short-term "collective

memory" to long-term history and collective memory means

that certain periods of the past are inflated while other periods

are compressed. We refer to this as "historical focusing."[151]

And, much like in our individual memories, it only makes sense

that we dismiss the less important memories and attend to

more significant shifts, just like how we forget what we ate a

week ago, but remember the births of our children. In most

U.S. history textbooks, for example, you will find certain eras

given greater attention and thereby time and space. More

often than not, the periods of history closer in proximity to the

present are given greater attention. The 1960s, for example,

might constitute a higher proportion of the textbook than did

---

[150] Eviaton Zerubavel, 40.
[151] Eviaton Zerubavel, 27.

the 1880s or 1830s. Those eras, however, might have more columns of analysis devoted to them than the 1710s or 1680s received. This whole process of inflating periods and compressing periods is a matter of interpretation and creates what Zerubavel has called "mountains and valleys."[152]

When Will This Debate Be Over? After Another Civil War?

So, let's return to that classic struggle between the African-American community and the pro-Confederate flag supporters in the American South. This is such a perfect case because it reflects so many of the dynamics between memory and history. Benedict Anderson says that modern nations' survival hinge on the paradox of that nation remembering the stories of national unity at the same time it is burying the nation's injustices. But for those who straddled the historical event, the paradox can be doubly painful. For African-Americans, the Civil War ought to have been a watershed event

---

[152] Eviaton Zerubavel, 29.

in their story. It unleashed the 13th, 14th, and 15th amendments. But, while slavery ended on paper in 1865, it did not change much of their everyday realities.[153] Slaves were subject to sharecropping, an abusive crop-lien system, and the wicked loophole in the 13th amendment that allowed for slavery "except as punishment for a crime whereof the individual has been duly convicted." In short, that loophole allowed a corrupt Southern criminal justice system to falsely arrest, prosecute, and convict African-Americans and then force them into chain-gangs where they returned to the fields and projects that had once occupied their lives under slavery. So, then Nathan Bedford Forrest and his fellow Ku Klux Klan founders raised the Confederate flag, it's not surprising that many African-Americans saw that flag as a symbol of a powerful and oppressive white force. And, because of the corruption in the Southern criminal justice system, it's also not surprising that

---

[153] I am consistently forced to remind my students that the Emancipation Proclamation of 1863 did NOT end slavery. It only freed those slaves being held in those states that were actively engaged in treason and had seceded from the Union. It was the 13th Amendment, passed in 1865, that ended slavery (on paper).

those same African-Americans came to distrust the police, the court system, judges and white authorities in general. The Confederate flag is a symbol of: 1) treason; 2) racism and oppression; and 3) corrupt law enforcement.

Now, to be fair, many white southerners have a different take on that story. Many saw Lincoln's election as an impending violation of states' rights and saw the Civil War as an act of "Northern Aggression." It means little to them that the states' rights they were afraid Lincoln would take away was the states' rights to enslave a portion of their population. Nor do they see the "Northern Aggression" as a response to Southern acts of war and secession. When the war was over, monuments and memorials were built to honor the many Southern men who lost their lives in that ugly, grisly war. But to honor the man does not mean that there is honor in the cause for which they fought. We can honor our veterans, but that does not mean that what they were told to do and ordered to do was just and right. I am by no means suggesting that we ought to have bashed Vietnam veterans when they returned, but our anger and vitriol ought to have been directed at their superiors and the Pentagon and the White House that ordered them to do what they did and ordered them to sacrifice their lives. The veteran is innocent. The cause is guilty. We should not have gone to Vietnam. Likewise, the fallen soldiers from the South in the Civil War can be honored for their loyalty and sacrifice, but what they were allegedly fighting for deserves no honor or monument. The Confederate flag for many southerners represents the honor of the man while for many of us, we see the flag as a symbol of that cause. Two different historical symbolisms attached to a single historical icon. As Zerubavel has noted, "For people struggling to maintain their identity against historical forces of conquest, oppression or dispersion, their (often mythical) past acquires great significance."[154] Here's where it gets important. BOTH the African-American community and the pro-Confederate flag southerners regard themselves in a struggle against historical forces of conquest.

---

[154] Irwin-Zarecka, 92.

African-Americans see that conquest at the hands of white southerners and white southerners see that conquest at the hands of the Union North. Perhaps, remembering their own pasts (as different as they may be) allows each group to be freely themselves. "The story of memory is, in the end," mal wrote, "the story of freedom."[155] But the question becomes does one's freedom include the right to wave symbols of oppression in the face of another? Sure it does—we call it the First Amendment. But, likewise, if a majority of any given electorate have chosen to have that symbol removed as a symbol of that population, so too then ought we abide by the powers of democracy. Keep the flag, wave it all you want, but it cannot represent a nation whereby all individuals fall under its power and governance. As Demosthenes once wrote, "what you wish for, you also believe to be true."[156] But that is the power of self-deceit. It overtakes what is "true" and replaces it with what we "want to be true" and, therefore, for us "is true."

---

[155] Malone, xi.
[156] Austin, 81.

Remembering to Build, Remembering to Purge

For some new nations, forging a new national identity was central to that nation's survival. We've probably all heard by now how Soviet historians tried to re-write their nation's past in order to serve the new fledgling nation and its ideals. It purged its past in order to build something new. And as noted, lots of nations have done this, the U.S. included. Ernest Renan has suggested that forgetting is critical to the creation of a nation.[157] I agree. I see nothing wrong in this re-interpretation of the past so long as debate is still allowed and fostered about that past.[158]

To have the debate (and not simply sweep it under the rug) is critical. Left unaddressed or unchecked, these types of conflicting "collective memories" can also prove dangerous. "Collective memory" in other parts of the world have led to revanchism or ethnic cleansing.[159] In Rwanda, for example, it

---

[157] Olick, 80.
[158] Olick, 13.
[159] Timothy Snyder, "Memory of Sovereignty and Sovereignty over

was the Hutus "collective memory" of the Tutsi's power and

collaboration with colonial powers, despite being a minority,

that led to that nation's civil war. It was "collective memory"

that stimulated the anti-Muslim sentiment in Bosnia-

Herzogovina and the subsequent genocidal acts there. You see

life is complicated. That complexity and the nuances that

accompany it make making decisions difficult and forming

consistent opinions a challenge. As Gordon notes, "to escape

from this cycle of ambiguity, some will latch onto visions of the

past that are simplistic, one-dimensional, and charged with

accusations against others."[160] It is far easier to blame someone

else than to take personal responsibility and analyze the

complex forces at hand. So—scapegoat the Jews, the Blacks,

the Muslims, the Tutsis, and so on and so on. In American

politics, history and memory have led to a further polarization

of the public.[161] Yet, as both individuals and as collectives, we

Memory: Poland, Lithuania and Ukraine, 1939-1999," in Muller, *Memory and Power in Post-War Europe*, 39.
[160] Gordon, 351. See also Olick, 21.
[161] Gordon, 353.

need a memory of the past to give us grounding in the present. In doing so, we get an "anchor" for our identity while we "nurture a vision of the future."[162]

Roger Bastide in his work *The African Religions of Brazil* suggests that "memories inherited from the ancestors survive only insofar as they can insinuate themselves into the existing frameworks of society."[163] In short, if the memory serves a purpose or offers a valuable lesson to those in the present, then the memory (or history) will persist. Just as remembering where the nuts and berries could be found served the hunter-gatherers, so too do certain memories serve a valuable function in modern societies, albeit more complex. Perhaps remembering the Holocaust will help us prevent another Holocaust. Perhaps remembering slavery will lead us toward true equality.

---

[162] Huyssen, 249.
[163] Olick, 162.

Therapeutic Forgetting

On the flip-side, perhaps forgetting slavery will allow us to move on (but I doubt it). But forgetting can be valuable.

We have in our heads millions of bytes of information, sensory input and fabricated thoughts based on that same input. Bergson wrote, "we mingle a thousand details out of our past experience."[164] It is difficult, and perhaps sometimes impossible, to interpret those memories correctly. They are simply too far gone. I experienced some traumatic events as a small boy. The details of those events, occurring over a span of at least five years, are so co-mingled within my brain that I am uncertain that I could ever unravel them. I certainly could never place an accurate chronology of those crimes, but I remember the perpetrators and their faces. I can see them because I have had a lifetime of seeing them. I have seen them in pictures and have myself re-told funny and happy stories involving them. I also know they are dead and so any full resuscitation of those

---

[164] Bergson, 24.

memories would be futile. What would I do with them that I have not done already? How might those memories serve me in a more constructive way today? Might the pain of "remembering" outweigh any beneficial impact today? Or, might it simply be best to purge those memories once and for all or to stuff them back into the dark recesses of my brain and hope they stay there? These are all questions beyond the purview of this book or any single psychotherapy session I may attend, but they are illustrative of the complexities of memory and the occasional need to dump certain memories to make room for better ones.

There appears to be other value in forgetting, however. In an earlier chapter, I introduced you to S. V. Sherashevsky, the memory trick artist, who amazed audiences in the Soviet Union throughout the 1930s. He had an incredible memory and acute sensory perception. Those attributes, however they may have been cultivated, also came at a cost. Sherashevsky, for example, struggled to hold down a regular job or handle the everyday burdens of daily life. He was, in many ways, incapacitated by his memory.[165] Likewise, Kim Peek had a

prodigious memory. It was reported that he could read two

pages simultaneously and remember both pages forever.

Forever. This is a remarkable task, but in certain other areas,

Peek was unfortunately limited. Peek ultimately served as the

real-life basis for the American film *Rain Man* starring Tom

Cruise and Dustin Hoffman.[166]

    The alteration of memories, the confused co-mingling

that occurs within all of our brains, may sometimes be referred

to as "secondary revisions."[167] In short, we sense something.

We receive sensory input. Thereafter, we recall those

memories by attaching it to or connecting it to a series of other

sensory input data. Bergson called it "borrowing." He said,

"memory...only becomes actual by borrowing the body of some

perception into which it slips."[168] This is the co-mingling of data,

the mixture of memories. So, think back to a pleasant moment

---

[165] Hutton, 28.
[166] Bloom, 98.
[167] Dowd Hall, 201, fn2.
[168] Bergson, 72.

in your life and conjure the details for that memory. It might be the cake you ate on your fifth birthday. You were surrounded by friends, wonderful decorations, smiling adults, a stack of presents, and a wonderful chocolate cake with pink frosting. Your memory of that cake might be that it was the best cake ever. Yet, that may not in reality be the case, nor any of the details you've recalled. The cake may have, in fact, tasted like cardboard but because of all the other pleasant circumstances in which it was enmeshed, you only now think or recall that it tasted good. The fact of the matter is that the whole experience may have been distorted in that way. You only want to remember the birthday as good because you have some attachment to that story. The kids may have been complaining about having to stay seated, the adults may have been frowning at their bratty children, your mother may have had a grimace on her face as she just realized she forgot an essential ingredient in the cake, and so on. But, in your memory, those bits of sensory data have been revised to accommodate your desires at a larger level. As Tyminiecka has noted about Jean-Paul Sartre's interpretation, "'waves' of memories come to us involuntarily. Sartre attributes them rather to the emotional order, stating that we not only do not choose when the memory manifests before us the interpretation of the past, it also affects our rational ability of deciding what should we do in future by reference to the 'completed,' 'finished' events of our life."[169]

Therapeutic Forgetting or Deliberate Deception through Historical Cherry-Picking?

As a crime historian I have had to wrestle with the complexities of gun ownership and its impact on crime. And while I have come to some intriguing conclusions which would surprise both those on the Far Right as well as those on the Far Left, I have noticed a sad development in American scholarship on the topic of gun ownership and the Second Amendment to the U.S. Constitution. In short, conservative scholars tended to approach the issue with a preconceived thesis and argument. In

---

[169] Anna-Teresa Tymieniecka, *Memory in the Ontopoiesis of Life.* New York: Springer Books, 2009, 151.

their efforts to support their predetermined position, they

claimed to have taken an "originalist" position. "Originalists"

are those Constitutional cherry-pickers who think they have

come to determine the "original" meaning and intent of the

Constitution.[170] Yet, overwhelmingly, these conservative

"originalists" are actually warping the historical facts, taking

them out of context, and applying them to their political

agenda. Ironically, those who have gotten the historical facts

and context right on this debate are those who have taken the

liberal position, but by virtue of their larger argument have had

to throw their own factual dominance out the window. The

liberal pro-gun regulation scholars have amassed significant

historical evidence to show that the conservative "originalists"

are full of baloney, but they have chosen instead to argue that

"originalism" does not actually matter given the profound social

---

[170] As a small boy, my mother took us into the migrant fields of western Oregon where we picked a whole host of crops. I remember vividly my mother teaching me the good ones to pick and the ones to leave on the vines. Constitutional cherry-pickers do the same. They find ripe pieces of evidence to suit their needs, but may leave all the remaining evidence (which counters their own argument) back on the vine. Historians try not to do that. Instead, we gather the evidence and then (and only then) do we form conclusions about the evidence.

change that has occurred in the last 226 years since the Bill of Rights was written. They suggest that although the Founders may have had one thing in mind it means little when citizens now are faced with grave danger from the private arsenals of wackos and that James Madison could never have conceived of the AR-17, AK-47, ground-to-air missiles or the whole host of other military-style weapons that the NRA would love for every American to have (or "bear").

Up until the 1980s, for example, the NRA was an association of sportsmen. They sponsored education on firearms and did not object to the first gun control measure taken in 1934, the National Firearms Act.[171] But, under highly funded advertising campaigns, the NRA was able to re-write history. In the 1990s, three NRA-endorsed pro-gun authors scribbled out over 30 articles twisting and warping the history of the Second Amendment to fit their ideological perspective. They were paid handsomely for their work; to the tune of over

---

[171] Michael Waldman, *The Second Amendment: A Biography.* (New York: Simon and Schuster, 2014), 88.

$1 million.[172] Those authors appear to have co-mingled their vision of what they wanted with what they understood of the past (or they have outright lied).

Interestingly enough, one might speculate that EVERY memory is that way. Every single memory we have, which in turn means EVERY single thought, is distorted by a co-mingling of data and sensory inputs and manipulated to our own bodily desires. If that's the case then while there is one single reality (a concrete past), there can never be a single unified perception of that reality (interpretations of the past). It is as if reality is merely a construct of our brain and what has happened or is happening now will never be knowable in its truest form. This is what, perhaps, many professions seek to address. Media professionals and advertising executives hope to manipulate your senses in such a way, repeatedly over time, so that we all come to a single desire, motivation, or purchase. Historians, likewise, want us to come to a single unified understanding of

[172] Ibid., 98.

the past so that we might all learn from our past mistakes and then take corrective actions in the future. Historians' constant repetition of that past, the inadvertent co-mingling and revisions of that past, might also create what Halbwachs called the "imago" or idealized image. Might we remember it so well that we have idealized the past beyond what was real and truthful?[173] Historian Allen Megill suggests that "memory is a domain of obscurity; it is not to be trusted."[174]

But, we know the limits of our memories. As Gordon described, "Of all the human faculties, memory is the most tragic." He added "It is sufficiently vivid to remind us of our sorrows, yet insufficiently reliable to make us doubt ourselves when we would commemorate our achievements. We cannot discount memory, and we cannot count on it."[175] Yet, ironically, we as humans need it to survive.

---

[173] Hutton, 7.
[174] Olick, 196.
[175] Gordon, 340.

CHAPTER FIVE

Dreams, Memory, and the Art of Identity Imagination

Introduction

Dreams have long captured the human imagination--which is ironic because dreams are central to our imaginations. I have always had an interest in my dreams and have, perhaps because of my good memory, been able to recall my dreams fairly easily. A few years ago, however, I began an exercise. I started keeping a "Dream Journal." I did so for several reasons. First, I thought it might be interesting to look back at these odd stories taking place within my brain and revel in the sheer creativity and marvel of those experiences. Second, I wondered if there were patterns to my dreams. As a historian, I am always interested in seeking patterns to human behavior. Why not dreams? Third, I wondered if I might have better recall of my dreams if I wrote them down. The results have been astonishing. My dreams range from the mundane to completely insane. I do see patterns and repeated themes. And, I do remember *some* of them, but remarkably, even after writing them down and re-reading them, I recall very little and very few. More importantly, I began to recognize the complexity of dreams. For example, I can have "memories" in dreams that do not occur in my "real" waking world. I can dream in a dream. I can have experiences in a dream that are equal in their power to my memory and living experience as some waking-world experiences. It is for that reason that dreams constitute the third section of this book. Dreams are part of the human experience; central to the brain and its memory; and is therefore critical to our "past." Great writer, thinker, philosopher Voltaire may have agreed. He once wrote, "History consists of a series of accumulated imaginative inventions."[176] Was he right? Are our "pasts" merely the contrived and imagined and wishful events that we want to believe make us who we are? What other "real" pasts have we shed by the wayside and forgotten, refused to admit as powerful forces in

---

[176] Archer, 104.

our lives? What tiny little event changed us and, in doing so, changed the course of history, yet went unrecorded, unnoticed, and, as a result, lost to obscurity? Are our dreams as real as our living everyday events? Is our history shaped by what we dream? Patrick McNamara, director of the Laboratory of Evolutionary Neurobehavior at Boston University's Department of Neurology and the VA Medical Center in Boston asks, "Why would Mother Nature highly activate your brain, paralyze your body, sexually activate you, and force you to watch these dreams? Why?!"[177] It was that very question that motivated McNamara to conduct his lifetime work on dreams. "If you want to understand what makes us tick," McNamara claims, "you're going to have to look at dreams."[178] And the rationale here is that perhaps the co-mingling of thought, consciousness, memory and history might be untangled in the course of dreams. Might this be the piece missing from the human history puzzle?

---

[177] NOVA, "What are Dreams?" PBS Documentary.
[178] NOVA, "What are Dreams?"

The Ancients and Dreams

Long before there were histories written by objective professional historians, there were other storytellers who wove together the epic tales of their people and wove them together with their dreams to make Creation Myths. With the advent of writing, however, those storytelling shamans became more and more obsolete and they were increasingly replaced with written histories. Dreams, as a result, became an entity into itself. Dreams became more personal rather than something a community might interpret. By the time of the ancient Greeks, dreams were beginning to be perceived as altogether different creatures. Heraclitus, for example, could add little to the discussion about dreams other than to suggest that dreams were merely products of the mind. Now, Heraclitus' observation seemingly adds no substantive new material to our ancient understanding of dreams except that he (and I'm sure many before him) recognized the location of the dream. After all, it seems only natural to us to think of dreams in our head, but why? The answer is simple—sensory input and dreams ARE

located there. Hippocrates (469-399BC) stated "by day the soul

receives images and by night it produces them."[179] This seems

pretty simple, but it may be the closest to the truth. There are

many modern dream-neuroscience experts who suggest dreams

are just a random production of sensory images from previous

experiences. But, we'll get to them later. Hippocrates went

further, however, and suggested that dreams had prophetic

qualities and diagnostic properties. In short, he believed that

one might be able to predict the future by examining those

dreams and that solutions to our world's problems may lay

secreted in these mysterious night-time productions.[180]

Plato (427-347BC), in contrast, believed in the

"psychodynamic elements" of dreaming. In his *Republic*, he

stated "In all of us, even in good men, there is a lawless wild

---

[179] Christopher Dewdney, *Acquainted with the Night: Excursions Through the World After Dark*. New York: Bloomsbury Publishing, 2004: 165.
[180] Robert L. Van de Castle, *Our Dreaming Mind: A Sweeping Exploration of the Role that Dreams have Played in Politics, Art, Religion, and Technology from Ancient Civilizations to the Present Day*. New York: Ballantine Books, 1994: 64.

beast nature which peers out in sleep."[181] Over 2200 years

before Freud, Plato suggested that the dream held something

deep and secret (and perhaps dark too) about the individual

who held them. In Plato's *Theaetetus*, Socrates is described as

having a discussion with Theaetetus and asks what proof he has

that he was in a dream having a discussion or in a waking state

having the discussion. Theaetetus had no response. Even for

Plato, in the 4th century BC, the difference between memory

and dream was blurred and questionable.[182]

Aristotle's *Parva Naturalia* suggests dreams are mere

recollections or reflections upon the previous day's events.[183]

And the historian Herodotus, our professional discipline's

proverbial Founding Father, claimed that the people of

Telmessus specialized in dream interpretation. It was reported

that King Croesus, the last King of Lydia, consulted with these

peoples of southwest Asia Minor. Whether it's true or not

cannot be verified and to what degree their interpretations

---

[181] Van De Castle, 64.
[182] Van De Castle, 3-4.
[183] Dewdney, 165-166.

were accurate is also unknown. What it does tell us, however, is that even as late as this period, peoples throughout the world were still given to believe in the power of dreams.

At the height of the Roman Empire, we begin to see a shift in human understanding of dreams. Artemidorus (ca. 150AD) wrote a work entitled *Oneirocriticon* (or *The Interpretation of Dreams*).[184] Artemidorus' work, among other things, offered an interpretation of dreams such that each individual might interpret them to their own design and tailor them to their own circumstances. It was, in many ways, one of the first "dream manuals" that you can still see at Barnes and Noble or next to the *National Enquirer* in the check-out aisle. *Oneirocriticon* is actually a set of five books loosely organized. The first book, creatively known as Book I, addresses over 80 subjects from dreams about the body and its actions. It's a dream encyclopedia of sorts. Unit 52, for example, states that dreams involving tools that cut or divide represent

---

[184] Dewdney, 166. Please note Artemidorus' use of this title nearly 1800 years before Freud.

disagreements while tools that smooth represent and "end to enmities."[185] Book II deals with dreams involving objects and events in the natural world and Books III, IV, and V are a loose collection of miscellaneous topics. The last book also includes a section of sample dreams, verified by Artemidorus, as practice cases for he and his son as Dream Interpreters.[186] Now, there are several things to note here. First, what Artemidorus has done for us is to describe the symbolism of the day. They may or may not be accurate in what they mean in the dream itself, but he has given us historians in the future a glimpse into what "they" thought and what "they" perceived as "symbols" and "signs" in their world. The reason this is important is that symbols and signs change over the course of time. The power of certain words may wane over the course of history. The term "scalawag," for example, means little to us today. In fact, you might even imagine Grandpa calling you that as he chases you across the yard with his cane. In 19th century America,

---

[185] Van De Castle, 67.
[186] Van De Castle, 65-67.

however, that was a "fightin' word." If you called someone a

"scalawag" in mid-19th century America, you might end up with

a bloody nose.[187] Secondly, Artemidorus' work also suggests

that there was sufficient demand for the interpretation of

dreams. What was it that created that demand? Was it the

sudden affluence among the elite of the Roman Empire? Was it

the profound change brought by the expansion of that Empire

and the concomitant anxiety that came with social change?

Tertullian, a Carthagenian lawyer and Roman priest,

wrote extensively about dreams and would later be influential

upon the thinking of Thomas Aquinas. Tertullian argued that

the dream state proved the presence of the "soul" and the

immortality of man. He suggested that dreams emanated from

four possible sources: demons, God, the soul (or self), and some

ecstatic state.[188]

---

[187] Note that the term "Scalawag" was used by white Southern
Democrats to label and identify southerners who had defected to the
Republican Party in that period of U.S. History after the Civil War
known as the Reconstruction Era (1865-1876). The scalawag's partner
in crime, of course, was the Carpetbagger—another derogatory term
by white Southern Democrats for a Northern Republican who had
gone South and had invaded their territory.
[188] Van De Castle, 77-78; Steven F. Kruger, *Dreaming in the Middle*

Two hundred or so years later, we begin to see another change in the role of dreams. Whereas Romans had started to move away from the idea that dreams were a product of the supernatural, new Christians created an unique paradox about dreams and dreaming. On one hand, they helped revive the idea that dreams had supernatural qualities. Was the dream a conversation with God? On the other hand, they were deeply suspicious of the dreams itself. Might those mysterious dreams be the work of the Devil? In short, new Christian thinkers had superimposed questions about dreams upon their own vague ideas about their own faith, the afterlife, and other issues they relegated to the realm of Mystery.[189] For example, St. Jerome, a 4th century Christian, made an important translation that would affect that paradox. St. Jerome was chosen by Pope Damasus I to translate the Bible into Latin in 382 AD. He correctly translated the Hebrew word "anan" to "witchcraft", but on three occasions deliberately shifted the translation to

---

Ages. Cambridge: Cambridge University Press, 1992, 46.
[189] Dewdney, 166-167.

"interpretation of dreams." This was not an accident, but more of a statement about St. Jerome's time period than the period about which he was writing.[190] Ultimately because of that, Biblical Law and Canonical Law of the Catholic Church increasingly criticized dreambooks as the work of Satan.[191] Many of the scholars cited specific sections of the perhaps mistranslated Bible. Leviticus 19:26 says "Do not practice divination or sorcery" while Deuteronomy 18:10 reads "Who practices divination or sorcery, interprets omens, engages in witchcraft."[192] Any interpretation of omens, including dreams therefore, became suspect by the Church and could have dangerous repercussions. It should be noted that today, according to a Pew Research Center study, some 23% of Christians believe in astrology.[193]

---

[190] Van De Castle, 78-79. See Morton Kelsey, *Dreams: The Dark Speech of the Spirit.* New York: Doubleday, 1968, 159.
[191] Kruger, 10-13.
[192] Van De Castle, 79.
[193] "Many Americans Mix Multiple Faiths" Pew Research Center, 9 December 2009. Accessed www.pewforum.org/2009/12/09/many-americans-mix-multiple-faiths/. Last accessed 30 July 2015.

Nonetheless, a significant number of Christian scholars continued their work on dreams and dream interpretation. Macrobius Ambrosius Theodosius, a contemporary of St. Jerome, wrote *Commentary on the Dream of Scipio.* This influential work went through at least 37 editions before 1700 and, in doing so, revived the interest in dream interpretation.[194] In this work, Macrobius suggested that dreams could be divided into two categories: *insomnium* and *visum.*[195] Here Macrobius made a sharp distinction about the content of dreams. For those he characterized as *visum*, he argued that these dreams involved substantive imagination and a "misconstruction of reality."[196] These were, in effect, the wild dreams we sometimes experience where we might fly, see particular monsters, and so forth. Macrobius said that these types of dreams were part of a higher level of dreaming and, as such, were much more revelatory. Those dreams he labeled as *insomnium* were, in contrast, "generated out of the self's

---

[194] Van De Castle, 80.
[195] Kruger, 21.
[196] Kruger, 22.

recollection of its waking life" and were, as a result, a "completely mundane experience."[197] Given the controversial nature of dream interpretation in Christian society at that time, it's not surprising that Macrobius was careful to warn readers of the potential dangers. Macrobius specifically referenced the power of *Incubus* (a male demon) and *Succubus* (a female demon) to overwhelm weak practitioners.[198]

Synesius of Cyrene was another 5th century Christian dream interpreter. As the Bishop of Ptolemais, Synesius authored the work entitled *On Dreams*. Synesius argued that dreams allowed people to elevate themselves to a higher plane of thinking. It allowed them to ascend into a "superior region" whereby they might receive guidance from their Higher Power. Synesius saw dreams as opportunities for problem solving.[199]

The renewed interest in dreams and dream interpretation also stimulated the creation of medieval dream books. There were, for all intents and purposes, three types of

[197] Kruger, 21.
[198] Van De Castle, 80.
[199] Van De Castle, 75-76.

dream books. There were dream alphabet books which included random dream themes alphabetized for the convenience of the reader. There was little organization or analysis of the content of dreams beyond this simple list of topics. There were also dream lunar books which connected the dream's content to the phase sof the moon. Lastly, there were dream book interpretations that gave detailed analysis of specific dream contents.[200]

The growth in dream interpretation popularity only aroused the scorn of the Church. Fr. Gracian, confessor to St. Theresa, believed "it is a sin to believe in dreams."[201] Gracian saw dreams, according to Van de Castle, as a "hazardous nocturnal activity" where Satan lurked and "provided a bountiful hunting ground for inquisitors seeking evidence of Lucifer's cloven hoofprints."[202] Yet, Thomas Aquinas, one of the Church's greatest scholars, suggested that dreams brought

---

[200] Kruger, 8-9.
[201] Van De Castle, 83. See Frank Seafield, *The Literature and Curiosities of Dreams.* London: Lockwood, 1869: 105-107.
[202] Van De Castle, 83.

by God were certainly not unlawful.[203] Another two hundred years later, a German monk named Martin Luther reminded his flock that the debate on dreams was not over. Luther (1483-1546) said that sin was "the confederate and father of foul dreams."[204] And so, going into the modern era, the question as to the source and function of dreams had not been resolved.

Even among the once-levelheaded Americans, the dangers and powers of dreams seemed present. Joseph Smith, founder of the Church of Latter Day Saints (more commonly known as Mormons) was given his religious instructions through a series of dreams and visions. Smith suggested that "dream memories" were not ordinary memories, but "novel histories."[205] He used these memories and novel histories (via dreams) to create (or reveal) a new understanding of Christianity and, as a result, an entirely unique American faith. Robert Cross Smith (1795-1832), no relation to Joseph, was an English astrologer

---

[203] Van De Castle, 80.
[204] Dewdney, 167.
[205] Charles Stewart, "Dreaming and Historical Consciousness," *Historically Speaking,* January 2013, 29.

who wrote under the pseudonym of "Raphael." Smith was at the cutting edge of a new 19th century European "dream craze." He wrote *The Royal Book of Dreams*. Smith's work was an elaborate system of "ciphers" and "signs" used to decode the association between dreams and reality.[206] Both Joseph Smith and Robert Cross Smith's work with dreams, however, were born out of the profound social changes occurring in their respective nations. In the U.S., the nation was experiencing a rapid growth of the institution of slavery, massive waves of immigrants from Ireland and Germany, and rapid urbanization. These profound social changes prompted many Americans, in what would be known as the Second Great Awakening, to seek solace in more traditional ways, especially in their faith. This social change caused a religious revival. But, among these revivalists were those who legitimately (and less so) in the power of dreams. For Robert Cross Smith a series of similar forces compelled he and his followers to seek answers in

---

[206] To read more about the art of sephromancy, see R. C. Smith, *Royal Book of Dreams*. London: Effingham Wilson, Royal Exchange, 1830, 40-51. See also the work of Edgar Cayce.

dreams: overcrowding, disease, urbanization, and loss of traditional farmlands. Again, social change prompted these "dream thinkers" to seek solutions in their nighttime skulls.

Freud and His Foundations

Over the course of the 19th century a series of scholars, both scientists and others, began a new wave of thoughtful analysis of dreams and their import. Louis Ferdinand Alfred Maury (1817-1892), for example, regarded dreams as the sheer result of external stimuli. His initial research, was has now since been disproven, posited that dreams were simultaneous to specific stimulus. If one heard water dripping from a water spout outside the window while sleeping, water would naturally occur in the dream. For Maury, the most important element were the dream's visual components or "hypnagogic hallucinations."[207] Stimulated by some outside experience, Maury believed, the brain then tapped into "previously

---

[207] Allan Hobson, *The Dreaming Brain: How the Brain Creates Both the Sense and the Nonsense of Dreams.* New York: Basic Books, 1988, 32.

inscribed experience."[208] To a certain extent, Maury was right. Under some circumstances, certainly, the brain may be responding to certain outside stimuli, but it cannot be a direct response in all cases. Moreover, any dream imagery had to be dependent upon previous experiences, previous visuals, or a combination of already existing features. I can't say that I have had any remarkable dreams with dragons or monsters, but were I to have such a dream it would not be out of place to think that I fabricated the "monster" from pre-existing ideas about what might constitute a monster. Maury's ideas ran in sharp contrast to his contemporary rival, Marquis Marie Jean Leon Hervey de Saint-Denis. Saint-Denis was a 19th century scholar-aristocrat. He was famous for having kept a dream journal in which he transcribed in great detail the features of his dreams.[209] Saint-Denis noted that there were stereotypical memories encoded in dreams. He called these "clichés-souvenirs." For Saint-Denis

---

[208] Hobson, 34.
[209] Hobson, 35-36.

these were fundamental images being used in dreams for

specific features in life.[210]

Around the same period that Saint-Denis and Maury

were debating the nature of dreams, a series of physicians

began exploring dreams and would later deliver foundational

principles upon which Freud would build. Gotthilf Heinrich von

Schubert (1780-1860) was a German physician. In his work, *The*

Symbolism of Dreams, Schubert suggested that dreaming was

simply symbolic "picture language." Schubert argued that

dreams were hieroglyphic in that they were a linguistic

expression and that they expressed multiple meanings into one

image.[211] Those images, he believed, were universal. Unlike

Maury, Schubert was less interested in what caused dreaming

than he was what the dreaming meant. In short, Schubert

believed that with attention and analysis, humans might

ultimately be able to decipher and comprehend this mysterious

language.[212] Schubert was not alone in this thinking. Karl

---

[210] Hobson, 36.
[211] Anthony Stevens, *Private Myths: Dreams and Dreaming*. Boston: Harvard University Press, 1997, 31.

Schemer's *Das Leben des Traunes*, published in 1861,

emphasized the symbolism of dreams.[213]

Alexander Grant, under the pseudonym of Frank

Seafield, published his work on dreams in 1865.[214] That work,

The Literature and Curiosities of Dreams, suggested that dreams

had meanings attached to the dreamer's personality and

experiences whereby the dreamer incorporated their personal

fears, physical ailments, and anxieties into their dreams.

Seafield saw dreams as a means by which people could reflect

upon their waking day issues and then modify their life for the

better.[215] For Seafield, as would later be the case for Freud, the

maxim "In somnio veritas" rang particularly true. "Truth is in

sleep."

W. Robert was another late 19th century scholar who

was taking dream studies to a new level. Robert saw dreams as

"a somatic process sof excretion."[216] In the 1880s, Robert

---

[212] Van De Castle, 89.
[213] Van De Castle, 92.
[214] Van De Castle, 90.
[215] Van De Castle, 90-91.
[216] Mark J. Blechner, "The Analysis and Creation of Dream Meaning: Interpersonal, Intrapsychic, and Neurobiological Perspectives,"

believed that the mind simply had too many memories and ideas to hold and that dreams were a means by which the brain eliminated these excessive thoughts.[217] Robert's work was one of the early studies of dreaming from a biological purpose in that it examined the biological purpose of dreaming. But not all dream scholars were scientific in their approach. French biologist Yves Delage asserted in 1891 that dreams came from incomplete acts or suppressed interpretations of the past. Now, it is here that we begin seeing the formative influences upon Freud.[218] Some of the scholars, however, were still deeply rooted in the idea that dreaming contained the seeds or evidence of immorality. Delage's reference to suppressed emotions was just the tip of the iceberg. F. W. Hildebrandt believed that all dreams were traceable to the "chambers of one's memory."[219] He also believed that the "more impure the life, the more impure the dream."[220]

Contemporary Psychoanalysis 84 (1998): 181-194.

[217] Van De Castle, 99.

[218] Van De Castle, 98.

[219] Van De Castle, 99

[220] Herman Westerink, *A Dark Trace: Sigmund Freud on the Sense of Guilt.* Leuren: Leuren University Press, 2009: 48.

All of these 19th century thinkers would help lay the foundation for the greatest "dream thinker"—Sigmund Freud. Now, Freud himself often minimized the contributions of his predecessors in dream study and, in doing so, magnifying his own stature in the discipline. But, it's clear, he did borrow from others, but that he also made his own unique contributions to the field.[221] For example, not once did Freud cite or pay reference to the work of Frank Seafield. He admitted having read Hildebrandt and agreed that traces of sin and guilt co-mingled in the individual's dreams.[222] Freud frequently referred to Schemer and gave him rare praise. But, when their ideas coincided, Freud made special effort to obscure the passages from Schemer so that it did not appear to have pre-dated his own ideas.[223] Whether Freud deserves all this attention is not the intent of this work. In the end, Freud emerged as the face of dream analysis and psychoanalysis. Freud's work *Die*

---

[221] Van De Castle, 111-112.
[222] Westerink, 48.
[223] Irving Massey, *The Neural Imagination: Aesthetic and Neuroscientific Approaches to the Arts.* Austin: University of Texas Press, 2009: 38.

Tramdeutung has compelled us to interpret our dreams as reflections of our internal fears and desires.[224] He saw this as an opportunity for skilled diagnosticians to assist people, but he did not regard this as something that could be addressed fully by the existing medical community.[225] For Freud, dreams were a product of an individual's past. "For dreams," Freud stated, "are derived from the past in every sense."[226] But, that past (that history) that influenced the dreamer also shaped their conscious and subconscious desires. Dreams, therefore for Freud, were part of a larger "wish fulfillment."[227] Like his predecessors, Freud believed dreams were "brimming with symbols."[228] It was the psychoanalysts' job, as a result, to interpret those dreams and help the dreamer retrieve lost or suppressed memories.[229]

---

[224] Kruger, 1.
[225] Hobson, 51.
[226] Kruger, 3.
[227] G. William Domhoff, *The Scientific Study of Dreams: Neural Networks, Cognitive Development, and Content Analysis.* Washington, D.C.: American Psychological Association, 2003: 136; Peter Gay, *Freud: A Life of Our Time.* New York: W. W. Norton and Co., 1988, 107.
[228] NOVA.
[229] Hutton, 61.

Freud's work revolutionized the discipline of psychoanalysis and the field of psychology, but it did little to resolve the century-old question as to how dreams work, how exactly they were tied to the brain and memory, and why we dream to begin with.

The places of memory that may need to be stimulated, for whatever purpose, can be triggered according to Sigmund Freud through self-analysis of jokes, parapraxes (or what we call "slips of the tongue"), certain compulsive behaviors, and dreams. Dreams, Freud believed, were unique ways to tap into hidden or buried memories. Whether you buy into Freudian theory or not (which I largely do not), it is difficult to ignore the fact that dreams are composed, albeit in unique ways, of past memories and thoughts. As such, might these "dream memories" be equally instructive as to who we are and who we want to be as is history—that fabricated dream memory?

The Post-Freudian World of Dreams

After Freud's grand entrance onto the psychoanalysis stage (or his creation thereof), we begin to see whole host of new dream psychological theorists emerge. Carl Jung (1875-1961), for example, was a Swiss psychiatrist and psychotherapist introduced a dream theory that included a compensatory function. Jung, like Freud, believed that dreams allowed for certain areas in life and thought that were not adequately exercised, developed, or nurtured.[230] Dreams, Jung believed, allowed for that development. In short, when the conscious mind could not provide for the human, the subconscious found a way to serve that purpose. But ultimately at the heart of Jungian dream theory was the belief that dreams could only be understood through "conceptual metaphors" made while awake.[231] Let's be clear here, however, there is a significant difference between Freud's concepts of dreams as hazy psychopathological testimony and Jung's concepts of

---

[230] G. William Domhoff, *The Scientific Study of Dreams: Neural Networks, Cognitive Development, and Content Analysis.* Washington, D.C.: American Psychological Association, 2003, 145.
[231] Domhoff, 147.

dreams as transparent creations from the dreamer's imagination.[232] Again, dream theorists sought to understand what the function and content of dreams were. While that is a noble endeavor, it might also be useful to consider what their interpretations of those dreams tell us about them as historical subjects and what their concepts of content and function tell us about the particular societies in which they lived.

Another early follower of Freud was the Austrian psychologist Wilhelm Stekel. Stekel was an initial follower of Freud, but ultimately broke with Freud in 1912. Stekel suggested that dreams were simply a struggle between "good" and "evil."[233] Stekel intended this idea to be more than simply a process of "conscience," however. For Stekel, dreams were a product of the tensions brought by "anagogic trends" (or a person's lofty aspirations) and their "katagogic trends" (or their base sexual and egotistical impulses). Stekel's ideas, in many ways, seems to be a synthesis of Jung and Freud. It was on one

---

[232] Hobson, 65.
[233] Van de Castle, 181.

hand "anagogic" in that it was born out of the creative well-spring of the brain (Jungian), but also "katagogic" in that it was psychopathological (Freudian).

Nonetheless, Freudian psychopathological theories remained. Alfred Adler believed the absence of dreaming was a sign of a healthy psychological state. "Very courageous people dream rarely for they deal adequately with their situation in the day time," he said.[234] Adler, in short, saw dreams as a means by which the brain addressed unfinished business.[235]

Henri Bergson, a French philosopher, believed that waking life was, in fact, the tainted thought. Bergson argued that waking life required such a deep level of concentration and constant decision-making about the present and the world at hand and were swamped with memories and sensations that pure human sensation and sensuality was ultimately dulled.[236] "The perception and the memory which we find in dreaming," he said, "are, in a sense, more natural than those of waking

---

[234] Van de Castle, 178.
[235] Van de Castle, 179.
[236] Van de Castle, 6.

life."[237] In short, he believed that dreams, because they were void of conscientious thought and sensation, were purer and more in keeping with the human mind. The mind, he believed, was sewn together in a tight conscientious web and that when dreaming (or when insane), that web was loosened and the mind freely allowed to wander. "Relax this tension or destroy this equilibrium," he wrote, "everything happens as if attention detached itself from life. Dreams and insanity appear to be little else than this."[238] How that process actually occurred was never fully addressed.

By the middle of the 20th century, we also began to see individuals like Calvin S. Hall exploring content analysis of dreams and the "continuity between dream content and waking life."[239] The end results from Hall's elaborate studies were so striking to Hall that he referred to it all as the "continuity principle."[240] Another 20th century dream theorist, Medard Boss

---

[237] Van de Castle, 6.
[238] Bergson, 227.
[239] Domhoff, 145.
[240] Domhoff, 146.

(1903-1990) sought to forego all the existing dream theories and see exactly what could be learned from the dreams directly. "We cannot consider dreaming and waking as two entirely different spheres," Boss said.[241] While that approach has a certain noble intent, this existentialist strategy fails to recognize that a scholar can never ignore their previous learning regardless of how hard they try.[242] We are all, in one way or another, slaves to our past experiences and thoughts. Boss' approach itself, to forego previous dream theories, was a response TO previous dream theories. We also need to always be cognizant that scholars seek to establish their own name and reputation as a "pioneer" and so often leave the trodden path into the wilderness.

By the end of the century, a significant number of scholars were openly rejecting Freudian ideas about dreams. Michel Foucault, for example, rejected Freudian dream

---

[241] Van de Castle, 183.

[242] For greater discussion of existentialist philosophies on dreaming and more, see the works of Ludwig Binswanger (1881-1966) and those whom he influenced like Heidegger and Husserl. See Susan Lanzoni, "Diagnosing Modernity: Mania and Authenticity in the Existential Genre," Configurations v12 n1 (Winter 2004): 107-131.

interpretation because Freud gave little to no attention to the fact that dreams were linguistically structured and that the relationship between symbols within that linguistic exchange were never examined. Foucault would argue that to suggest a psychoanalyst could provide exhaustive analysis of such complex dream terrain was absurd. For Foucault, instead, dreams were life. "In dreams," he wrote, a person "encounters what he is and what he will be, what he has done and what he is going to do, discovering the knot that ties his freedom to the necessity of the world."[243] Foucault was not the first to suggest the intimacy of dreams and reality. Havelock Ellis, a half-century earlier, suggested something similar. He suggested that the "opaque curtain between the present and future can also be drawn aside when we take a seat as a spectator in the nocturnal theatre of dreams."[244] It is, Ellis wrote, "the charm of dreams that introduce us into a new infinity."[245] He further

---

[243] Charles Stewart, "Dreaming and Historical Consciousness," *Historically Speaking*. January 2013, 28. See Michel Foucault, "Dream, Imagination, and Existence," in Binswanger, ed. Keith Hoeller (Humanities Press international, 1986), 47.
[244] Van de Castle, 7.
[245] Van de Castle, 7.

added that through dreams "the fetters of civilization are loosened."[246] Dreams were an avenue for creativity and innovation.

The Science of Dreams

Over the course of the second half of the 20th century, neuroscientists began making serious and systematic scientific studies of dreams and dreaming. In 1939, Nathaniel Kleitman's publication of *Sleep and Wakefulness* marked the emergence of modern sleep research. By the 1950s, the notion that sleep was simply an opportunity for the brain to rest was dispelled.[247] While they are not yet done and the complexities of the brain still serve to deliver challenges to the scientists, some of their early conclusions seem, on the surface, pretty simple. Jessica Payne and Lynn Nadel state, "dreams reflect a biological process of long-term memory consolidation serving to strengthen the neural traces of recent events, to integrate these new traces

---

[246] Van de Castle, 6.
[247] Hobson, 163-165.

with older memories and previously stored knowledge, and to maintain the stability of existing memory representations in the face of subsequent experience."[248] On the surface, that seems all fine and dandy, but there are some important questions that ought to be explored with reference to that statement. For example, if dreams are tied to "recent events" then why do those events not display themselves as they were or are rather than the fantastic, imagined scenarios that play out in our heads? If dreams are tied to memory, as they suggest, why can we not remember our own dreams? Why do, we for all intents and purposes, suffer dream amnesia?[249] How can memory be strengthened and why does it manifest itself in these unusual stories?

Perhaps then a slightly more detailed understanding of dreams might be of value. We now know that dreaming occurs, generally, in two phases: REM sleep and Non-REM sleep.

---

[248] Payne and Nadel, 671
[249] Hobson, 213-214.

Non-REM: Reviewing and Making Sense of the Past

Non-REM sleep, which is not a very creative name, involves little to no rapid eye movement (or REM). Non-REM sleep is what has been called "slow-wave sleep" as our brains undergo much slower brain-wave activity. Non-REM sleep occupies about three-fourths of the sleep that occurs at night.

When we engage in non-REM sleep at night, our brain is still dreaming. It is not being revealed to us in episodic fashion as we will discuss later, but in short condensed blips. It's as if the brain is giving us a short trailer to a movie. There is no real substantive connection to the blips (on the surface), but they are connected to our thoughts and memories nonetheless. Matt Wilson of MIT explains that "during non-REM sleep the brain is taking the past and trying to figure out how it might relate to the future."[250] It's, in effect, doing what I do in the classroom (or as I prepare for my lectures). It's trying to find and make connections that make the information useful and valuable to its audience. Both the works of Deirdre Bennett of

---

[250] NOVA.

the Harvard Medical School and Sara Mednick suggest that

dreams allow us to make freer and more creative associations.

If critical thinking is, in part, seeing and recognizing patterns,

then perhaps dreams allow us a vantage point where we might

see a wider scope of patterns. It's almost as if dreams elevate

us from the forest floor where we can only see the trees and

raise us well above the canopy of that forest so that we can see

the forest itself and how that forest relates to other geographic

features.[251]

REM: Using the Past to Make Good Decisions in the Future

In 1953, scientists discovered what we now know today

as REM, or rapid eye movement, a distinct phase in an

individual's sleeping process.[252] Nathaniel Kleitman and Eugene

Aserinsky noticed unique sleeping brain patterns. Using an

electroencephalograph, scientists like Kleitman and Aserinsky

were able to measure the electrical waves of the brain during

---

[251] NOVA.
[252] Hobson, 13.

sleep.[253] There are some scholars who believe that REM is not, in fact, a phase of sleep. Instead, they argue that REM is, in fact, a waking state but where the individual is paralyzed and overcome with hallucinations.[254] Either way, in the last 62 years, we have come to a far more complex understanding of this REM stage. We know, for example, that among premature infants, REM constitutes roughly 75% of their sleep. The average normal baby is caught in the REM stage only 50% of the time and by adulthood it drops down to only 25% of the sleep period.[255] It may very well go even lower as the individual ages through latter periods of adulthood. This might suggest that dreaming in children is connected to the "development of the neural network for spatial construction" while adult dreaming has more to do with that neural network's "maturation."[256]

REM is a critical phase in the dreaming process for it is here that the bulk of the connected, storyline dreams we

---

[253] Ernest Hartman, "Dream," *World Book Encyclopedia,* 1978, 279.
[254] William C. Dement, *Some Must Watch While Some Must Sleep.* 1972, 26.
[255] Dement, 30
[256] Domhoff, 5.

experience occur. In fact, an interrupted REM stage may allow for the most "vivid dream recall."[257] It appears at this date that the forebrain is generating the REM and, in doing so, helping shape the dream content.[258] According to Evans, during the REM stage, neural pathways used in everyday thinking and operating become isolated and, in doing so, expose themselves for self-modification and reorganization. This is, in effect, allowing for the plasticity of the brain and memory.[259] Because the brain patterns are following specific synaptic routes and are being modified along the way through this loop, the REM phase dreams come to us as episodic stories. There is an explicit storyline involved in REM dreams, as fantastic as they may be. This will be in sharp contrast to non-REM dreams which unfold in our brains as short condensed blips. This difference is important. While non-REM sleep, as I've indicated earlier, was trying to make useful connections, REM sleep is now trying to make useful hypothetical applications. Matt Wilson from MIT

---

[257] Dement, 37-38; Hartman, 279.
[258] Domhoff, 10.
[259] Doidge, 239.

further explains, "in REM it's actually trying to experience the future, move into the future."[260] In short, the brain is testing its own hypothesis. REM sleep allow humans without risk to test the possibilities. It allows us to reach our maximal level of potential without the peril associated with it in waking life.

It is perhaps because REM sleep is a rehearsal phase that during that phase our muscle tone is reduced and we become "functionally paralyzed." Our brain shuts our bodily response system down so that when we practice the "fight or flight" in our dreams, we don't actually flee, punch someone in the nose, or flail at a partner beside us.[261]

It's also in the REM phase that negative experiences within dreams occur. Many scholars have suggested that this is because of the active role of the amygdala in the REM phase. The amygdala is a small section of the brain where negative flight or fight emotions are stored and are central to the

---

[260] NOVA. It is worth noting here that the difference between REM and Non-REM with regard to episodic content and blips is not entirely complete. There is some episodic content in non-REM, but not as much as in REM. And, the amount of episodic content in REM diminishes late in the REM phase. See Pay
[261] Hartman, 279; NOVA; and Hobson, 150.

functioning and survival of our species.[262] Brain scans have ultimately revealed that when we dream, the emotional center of our brain is not only active but so too is the areas essential for sexual, survival, and aggressive instincts.[263]

Now I am about to propose an idea for which I have no evidence. I have no science behind this idea. I have no studies, no secondary literature, nothing. It is purely an idea born out of the creative recesses of my brain (and perhaps a dream). In the Middle Ages, as Francis Yates has so adeptly demonstrated, individuals used complex theatre-like constructions to remember things. By constructing a visual structure with rooms and compartments and the like, the medieval thinker could use that mental spatial configuration as a framework for remembering a whole host of things. So, to remember lines for a play, they might create a story whereby they move through rooms in the structure in a particular order and, in doing so, cue the specific lines of that Shakespearean production. This is an

---

[262] NOVA.
[263] Doidge, 239.

old, but complicated, memory trick. I have employed the trick myself when playing with my children the old game "I am going on a trip and I'm taking...." But, if we work on that premise that a structured environment might serve as a framework for memory and that certain things might also be symbols for other things within that environment, then might REM sleep be a framework memory system for our brain. So, for example, might my entry into a hotel lobby (which is a frequent recurrence in my dreams) hold the framework for a larger memory storage idea that has little (if anything) to do with the hotel. In short, might the story we see appear in our dreams simply be the vehicle for a memory storage process?

Just as I created a strange little story through a variety of mnemonic devices to remember the Kentucky Derby, our brain does the same for more complicated, perhaps unrelated information. The difference is I KNOW the difference between the remembered material (the horse's names) and the memory structure storyline. In dreams, perhaps, we have yet to be able to distinguish between the remembered content and the bizarre story upon which it was saddled. But, what do I know?

All in all, dreams are clearly associated with memory. Robert Stickgold, a dream expert, has gone so far as to say that dreams and sleep "refine the memory; improves the memory; it makes the memory more useful for the future."[264] So, if memories are critical to our survival as a species (whether that is to remember where to find nuts and berries as hunter-gatherers or remembering to pick up our kid at baseball practice lest we suffer the wrath of an angry wife), then it appears dreaming is central to that memory capacity. If so, then dreams are essential to our survival as well.

The Biology?

Where does this brain activity of dreaming occur? It occurs generally in a closed loop between the associated cortices, paralimbic structures, and limbic structures.[265]

---

[264] NOVA.
[265] Domhoff, 16

Because this loop involves the medial frontal cortex, the

anterior cingulate cortex, and the orbital-frontal cortex, "the

conceptions and concerns of waking life" are loosely integrated

into the dream itself.[266] So, dreams then are actually born from

the confluence of sleep and consciousness.[267] Harvard scientists

McCarley and Hobson suggest that the brain stem's stimulation

of those cortices, however, help account for the "chance

manner" of dreams and the subsequent looping of the dream

through those cortices allows the brain to try to make sense of

those random thoughts. In short, it's as if the mind experiences

a looping of ideas that allows the random synaptic firings to be

refined, defined, and explained through a host of other neural

networks.[268] Their landmark 1977 paper proposed what has

become known as the "activation-synthesis model of dream

production."[269] Not long thereafter, in 1983, Francis Crick (of

DNA fame) suggested that dreams are nothing but "cognitive

---

[266] Domhoff, 16-17.
[267] Domhoff, 6.
[268] Hartman, 280
[269] Maury M. Breecher, "The Biology of Dreaming: A Controversy That Won't Go to Sleep," (http://www.columbia.edu/cu/21stc/issue-3.4/breecher). Last accessed 15 July 2015.

debris" and that we dream to forget.[270]   Both works thoroughly

renounce the work of Sigmund Freud.[271]

So, if thoughts are simply long extended strings and intricate webs of synaptic connections that form "ideas" and are stimulated by input and filtered along pre-existing connections, then might memories simply be old traces of synaptic connections modified by new thoughts. If so, might dreams be old memories freely firing along synaptic patterns? Might dreaming be the path of least resistance as synaptic firings lay unfettered by new sensory input and conscious thought.

The Art

For Havelock Ellis, as you may remember, dreams allowed a "new infinity." That new infinity, for some, meant experiences beyond their own waking life. This has been the case for me. Ten years or so I woke from a deep sleep and immediately recalled the dream I had been experiencing. In

---

[270] Breecher, 1.
[271] Kruger, 1.

that particular dream I had been both a participant and an observer, a phenomenon that I have experienced on many occasions. The dream flowed almost like a movie and in this dream I had been saved from the Nazis on the night of Kristallnacht in November 1938. I had been saved by a little girl and her family and only allowed to come out from my hiding place and into the fresh air of the family's courtyard when under the cover of darkness. After many years living in hiding and serving as the family's butler, I was forced to take the little girl, now an adult woman, to a hospital to save her life. I had never been told that the Nazis were out of power or that the war was over. I was living as an adult man in Germany under the fraudulent belief that I might be killed were I to be discovered.

The dream sat in my brain and over the course of the ten years more and more details were filled in. It was not that I had forgotten elements of the dream, but that my mind was manufacturing elements to fulfill the larger story. In the summer of 2015, as my cancer grew in my lungs, I finally wrote the story down and it flowed out of me effortlessly into nearly

200 pages. When I wrote the last section of what is tantamount

to a novel, I almost cried. I cried because I felt what the little

boy felt and I was sad that it was over, that the memories of

that existence, the details he harbored in his fictional life, were

now over. I have re-read the manuscript many times since then

and am constantly amazed that this story was not, in fact, real

but born out of the dreams streaming within my head.

Moreover, I came to realize that there were so many details,

nuances within the story, that actually had been features of my

real past. I had forged them together into a single whole and

they felt real and they changed me. The experiences of the

main character were mine. It was as if I had survived the story,

undergone that great deception, and so forth. It's hard to

answer the next question as it is like the proverbial "chicken or

the egg?" Was the empathy that I further developed from that

dream born IN the dream? Was it a product of having

experienced via the dream's character and storyline? OR, was

the empathy I further fostered the motivating force behind the dream? Did, in fact, the empathy I had already nurtured over the course of my life compel me to empathize with Holocaust victims so deeply and profoundly that I dreamt of their pain and felt their pain? I am not sure there will ever be an answer to that question, but as I reflect upon it I can only conclude that it is, in fact, BOTH. I had empathy for the Jewish story before I dreamt the dream, but it was further enhanced after having had the dream. That's not so unusual, after all. It is how the brain works. The brain is a self-reinforcing mechanism. The more you use your brain, the stronger it becomes. The less you use it (or even use it in less than novel ways), the less strong the brain becomes.

The creativity of that whole Kristallnacht experience was born in my dreaming brain. It is as Hobson calls an "autocreative" process.[272] For Hobson, that creativity seems completely explainable. "The internally generated signals," Hobson writes, "are not only synthesized into extraordinary stories but are also accepted as experiential reality. The reason

---

[272] Hobson, 17.

is that there is no external input to structure experience, and that only remote memory serves as a reference point."[273] For Hobson, this makes dreaming delusional.

False Memory (Waking Dreams?):

In 2015, Republican presidential candidate Donald Trump stated on the campaign trail that he remembered watching Muslims in New Jersey celebrate the collapse of the World Trade Centers in New York City. There's a difference between a lie and an honest mistake. However slight, it's a crucial distinction in politics, and especially in the campaign of Donald Trump. He insisted that he had watched news footage of "thousands of thousands of people" celebrating the terrorist attack as if it were a good thing. He noted that New Jersey had a large Arab population. Yet, no one has yet to find any evidence that there was any news footage of that sort or that any celebration ever occurred in New Jersey. Trump's account, on the surface, appears to have been a bold-faced (and that

---

[273] Hobson, 212.

may be true). But as coverage of Trump's seemingly crazy

assertion spread some psychologists were interviewed and

testified that Trump may have unconsciously fabricated the

memory of the Arab celebration of 9/11 and that this

phenomenon is not unique to Trump and, in fact, occurs all the

time.

Deryn Strange, a psychologist at the John Jay College of

Criminal Justice in New York, stated "... my research, and the

research of my colleagues, certainly supports a more charitable

interpretation: that this is a false memory." Under the right

circumstances and with a powerful suggestion, Stange

suggests, people can conflate their memories such that they

legitimately believe that something has occurred when it

actually has not. In short, Trump may have conflated the

celebration of a few radical Muslims (images of which were

repeated over and over on many major networks) with the

stories of Muslims in New Jersey. When confronted with the

mistake, Trump held doggedly to his story. "It was on

television. I saw it," Trump told Stephanopolous, "They were cheering as the World Trade Center came down."[274] In this

case, memory did not reveal the truth, but to a certain degree

the desired "truth" that fit Trump's narrative for his vision of

the nation. The historical evidence, the memory of that

historical event, and the dream of what that memory might

mean all converged in just another crazy episode along the

Trump campaign trail. But, Trump's campaign was not a dream.

It was a nightmare.

The Reason

I have no recollection of my birth, no memory of any

particular day apart from a few special days marked by "anchor"

events like tragedies or remarkable occasions. I can tell you

where I was on 9/11, my daughter's births, and when I found

out about my cancer. I cannot tell you which wedding

[274] Max Ehrenfreund, "Why Donald Trump may think he saw people cheering on 9/11," The Washington Post, 24 November 2015. Online accessed   24 November 2015, http://www.msn.com/en-us/news/politics/why-donald-trump-may-think-he-saw-people-cheering-on-9-11/ar-BBno2BU?li=BBnbfcL&ocid=HPCDHP.

anniversary it was where we went to a Scandinavian Festival in Junction City, Oregon and drank Pyramid Apricot Ale. I know I went to a beer festival with Steve Malany along the Portland waterfront, but could not tell you the moth or day, let alone the year. I know in 1975 I formed a club to collect hot wheels and that same Steve Malany paid his dues. I bought a green car, but when? And, most of the days of my past fall into obscurity. They are lost. Yet, there are dreams I can recall with vivid detail. I cannot remember what I had for lunch yesterday, but I remember the dream of driving a van through Bozeman, Montana and taking a sharp left turn onto a road into the mountains. I can remember a whole host of dreams and yet I do not count them among the experiences that have shaped me.

Some scholars have suggested that dreams allow our brains the opportunity to create hypothetical dangers so that we are better prepared for the "real" ones when they do occur. This is also in keeping with the thoughts of some memory scientists. Ingvar, for example, theorized that memory was central to an individual's construction of "alternate hypothetical behavior patterns in order to be ready for what may happen."[275]

Still others have suggested that dreams are the first articulation of what the body already knows. In the mid-19th century, for example, M. Macario classified those dreams heralding an onset of an illness as "prodromic." As late as 1983, Bernard Siegel, via the *Dream Network Bulletin*, announced a prognostic prodromal dream of metastatic cancer in one of his patients.[276] I have not yet had a single recorded dream associated with my own cancer. I certainly do not recall having one before my diagnosis. Yet, here I am.

The Question

Does our inability to incorporate dreams into the meaning of our lives, into the fabric of our existence and our meaningful past somehow suggest its irrelevant? Or, is it that we have unwittingly divorced ourselves from the value of that

---

[275] Szpunar, 1.
[276] Van de Castle, 365-366.

portion of our brain? Have we simply said "dreams are not real and thus are not important." Race is not real either, but the concept has been critical to our nation's history. Perhaps the dream has greater importance than we realize or credit it. Perhaps we have deeper meanings to the planet and to one another that are embedded in our dreams.

My dreams shape me. They give me escape. They have taught me some coping skills and have inspired me, rested me, challenged my assumptions of the world, and in many cases, gotten me back on track. They have also given me fodder for thought and creative approaches to classroom challenges. I've written one novel based on a dream and am initiating a second base don another. Dreams can be compelling forces in our lives. So, the question remains...if our thoughts for 16 hours a day are so valuable, why aren't the thoughts of our brains in the last 8 hours also of value?

I'd ultimately argue that dreams are of value; great value. The problem is that we have not yet had the ability to openly discuss them, what they might mean, and what value they have in our modern society. It's as if we have kept the "dream" a private personal video in our head and have been afraid to talk with our friends and family about them. It is in the process of discussion and reflection that we might gain greater insights into our dreams and therefore into ourselves. To discuss our dreams with others might be too scary or frightening. How does an adult woman, for example, tell her husband that she had a dream in which she was intimate with President Abraham Lincoln on the floor of her old high school gym? How does he tell her that he had the same dream? Does anyone really want to admit their deepest and darkest fears? Do they want to expose the uncontrolled inner workings of their own brain? They might not want to, but perhaps it would be good for us all if we had open and frank discussions about who we are and what we think and believe. Perhaps dreams might afford us the context for that reflection and discussion. I would further argue that it is in that reflection process that we can begin to disavow ourselves of false beliefs and eliminate (or let go of) our fears. I had a dream the other night that I was running down a corridor at my university. When I awoke I

realized how much I missed running or moving about with any

agility. The cancer, after all, had involved the removal of my

femur and I have yet regained the strength I once had or the

ability to fully bend or straighten my left leg. I hobble about

with a cane. So, when I awoke I was saddened. I longed for the

days that I could move so freely. But, those days, for now, are

gone and I have to accept where I am and what I can do. There

is no way to fully measure how that longing had affected me

before the dream and likewise there is no full way to determine

the impact of that self-realization. It is fair to say, however, that

I AM changed the more I become self-aware. So, now I dodder

across the campus very slowly, I enjoy the wind across my body,

and feel the sun across my face. I enjoy smelling the proverbial

"roses."

CHAPTER SIX

Teaching: History, the Art of Connections, and the Human Brain

Ironically, this section poses the greatest difficulty in writing for me. First, I am already a self-proclaimed unorthodox historian in that I question the very values and claims most within my discipline make, namely the assertion of "objectivity." But, secondly, I have never taken a course in education, teaching, or pedagogy in my entire life. Given another book, I could rail at that discipline as well. Instead, I will simply say that everything I learned as an "educator," I learned from the masters with and by whom I was trained and through a painful, but rigorous trial and error. I have, however, after nearly 20 years in the classroom, come to some observations that may be worth noting and sharing about the teaching of history as a subject. I will, as a result, in this chapter highlight general educational principles that I feel are important (and professional teachers and those crazy Ed.Ds can criticize this in their own works) and then some specific tricks for history. I will even offer some tricks for both general survey courses as well as specific upper-division classes. The general educational observations and tricks include: Organization, Know Your Audience, Connections with Students, Connections with Material, Assignments as Instruction, Empowerment, and Fun. I will call these the Ultra-7.

This is not purely a section devoted to the practitioner. That is not my intent. What I hope you will discern, as we move through this section, is that the brain and our memory and our dream functions are aligned in similar ways. I hope you will see the pattern by having moved through the pattern. So, bear with me and keep your eyes open. Or, I suppose you could if you were a dimwit, move to those sections that on the surface seem more intriguing to you.

Organization

This seems blatantly obvious. Anyone teaching history needs to be organized. But, I am not simply talking about having a syllabus or knowing in advance what you intend to lecture upon, although those are also important. Instead, I'm suggesting that there be thoughtful, reflective attention given to the creation of that syllabi and how the course is both implicitly and explicitly organized. For example, I have had colleagues in both my discipline and others who have simply created a list of topics that they thought every student ought to know before leaving that course. Some have actually referenced the course objectives and outlines, but many instructors simply create a list and then count the number of days. If they had too many topics for the number of days allowed, they consolidated topics. On the other hand, if they had more days slated than topics identified, they scavenged their old texts for new additional topics to fill-in. This is, for all intents and purposes, horrible instructional planning. Were I to simply create a list of historical subjects I think they need to understand, I will have missed the opportunity to reach out to these students. Moreover, there is an assumption in that planning that YOU know what subjects are important, THEY don't know any of the subjects you've identified, and that (by virtue of the allotted days) all topics are of equal value.

Instead, I recommend that every instructor review what the overall objective of the course is and to develop specific objectives for each topic and clearly identify for both one's self and the student, how these objectives will be met and the value of that specific organization. With reflection, an instructor may realize that the course's traditional organizing principles were not effective or efficient in educating the student. They may realize that there are better ways to impart the information and skills.

Organization also requires us think of the larger flow of information and allows us to build upon a student's blossoming knowledge base and skills set. All of this, as noted above, ought to be shared in a syllabus. This again seems obvious, but there are thousands of instructors nationwide who have foregone this simple document. The syllabus is not only a guide for the student as to what topics will be covered and a list of information that ought to be of value—office location, hours, contact information, required reading, test schedule, and so on. The syllabus is also a contract. I see it as a binding contract between myself and my students. It tells them, first and foremost, that I am the instructor on record and that I have the integrity to identify how grades will be allocated and for what assignments they will be employed. If a student has a grievance about my grading, it will have to be based on something apart from perceptions of an "A" and calculation errors. Instead, the student will know up-front what is expected of them and the consequences for failure.

I also see this syllabus as another opportunity to educate. In short, the syllabus does two things. First, it requires the student to be attentive and responsible. If I can invest time and energy into creating the syllabi, then it is their challenge to master its requirements and understand my position. This is not typically an objective for the course, but most teenagers (as is the case with my students generally) need gentle lessons on independence, responsibility, and accountability. Secondly, the syllabus is a pedagogical tool. A student can learn the basic chronology from the course lecture schedule I include. They can decipher the importance of specific lectures by reading the lecture objective. In doing so, they are one small step closer to fulfilling the course goals than their classmates who have not (or will not) read that administrative document.

Know Your Audience

Many instructors often forget that the wide-eyed faces sitting in front of them are college students. They are teenagers and they come to the classroom with their own unique set of circumstances. Some are non-traditional students (whom I refer to as the Older-than-Average students) who may have the same knowledge base as their pimply-faced classmates, but have a whole host of experiences and "baggage" that are worth considering in the course of instruction.

Many instructors forget this. They think students "know" the base information or "ought" to know that information. The fact is, however, that many of our students don't know what we want them to know before entering our classes. Frankly, I'm not convinced it's their fault. Nor am I suggesting that their high school instructors failed them either. What I am suggesting is that there is no such thing as a "problem student." If a student doesn't know (or remember) the information Mrs. McGillicuddy taught in the 3rd grade OR doesn't recall the information Mr. Potratz allegedly taught in the 8th grade OR wasn't taught by Coach Schmucker in the 11th grade, is it really their fault and ought blame even be identified? The fact remains that they are in MY class NOW and I have an obligation to get them to the next stage. I do not subscribe to the idea that I will simply do my dog and pony show and everyone must understand it and like it and that I will grade you on skills that I may have not even addressed in class. Instead, I see it as my obligation to help every student get to the highest possible place in understanding and skill development within the given time period (usually 10-15 weeks).

Many instructors will have students that will pose challenges to their traditional teaching strategy. They may be physically disabled, learning disabled, emotionally immature, prone to gang or thug mentality, or genuinely disinterested. It is my challenge then to reach each of those disparate groups, adjust or modify my course to accommodate them, and bring them back fully into my original objective. For the physically disabled, most university have accommodation forms and protocol. Edinboro University, where I teach, has a disproportionately high number of disabled students, but has in place a process to work with them. Even then, I find my accommodations to be more effective. For example, if a student has been diagnosed with a learning or physical disorder

that allows them more time for exams, rather than schedule a

separate exam time and a testing facility, I simply require those

students to complete a take-home exam that is typed, double-

spaced and clean of any typographical errors and the like. I can

do this because I realize that the real objective of the exam has

less to do with ambushing the student on specific information

as it does in compelling them to write a clear thesis, use

substantive specific evidence, and be clear and concise in their

writing. The take-home exam doesn't compromise this.

Connections with Students

On the surface, this tip seems to replicate the previous

idea that an instructor ought to know their audience. I would

argue, however, that there is a distinct difference between

knowing who you are speaking to and connecting with that

same body. For the purposes here, I recommend that any

instructor for a meaningful relationship between the students and themselves. Study after study at the higher education level will tell you that access and strong relationships with faculty are one of the most important factors in college student success. I'm not suggesting hugs and kisses and absolute familiarity. On the contrary, but the student needs to feel as if they are part of the process and that the faculty knows who they are and that they matter in the educational endeavor. It is for this reason that I learn all of my students' names on the first day of class. Yes, some 300+ students' names are learned the first day. I even tell my students explicitly why I do this: when a student knows they are known and that they matter in a college class, they will do better. It has less to do with their self-esteem, in my opinion, as it does that they know there is a faculty who cares, knows who they are, and can call on them. Likewise, they believe that any faculty who goes so far as to learn their name must be a faculty for whom they can trust. My students, as a result, will often turn to me for guidance and advice in matters beyond my own course material. Moreover, many students who now trust me will often heed my advice and become

History majors. They know that I care and that I would not steer them down a wrong alley. Moreover, knowing a student's name heightens the standard. Students in my classes know that because they are not anonymous, they might be called on in class. As a result, they must come to class prepared. Students also know that because I know their names, I might see them outside of class. I warn them that if they choose to skip class, they had better have a good reason or remain hidden behind their dorm room doors. If, on a day that they have skipped, I am driving down the street and I see them sitting on the stoop of "The Empty Keg" (a local bar), I will most likely roll down my car window, call them out by name, and remind them when their next class is. When that has happened (which is rare), I am always happy to see the next class when they sheepishly enter the classroom and take their seat. I am not sure how any instructor can expect high quality work out of students who are completely nameless to that instructor.

But my recommendation for "connecting" with students also includes recognizing that students have issues outside of your classroom. I may be arrogant, but I would never think that the most important thing in my students' lives are the 50 minutes they spend with me three times a week. I understand they have family, work, and a whole host of complicated human life issues swirling around them. This is particularly true of my students at Edinboro University where a significant proportion are older-than-average commuter students. How can any compassionate professor dismiss the challenges of dealing with small children before an 8am class? How can we dismiss the grief suffered by a student with the passing of a grandparent? How can we dismiss the general stress of life when we ourselves are often caught in that same maelstrom? In short, be sensitive to your students and understand that the information you deliver on any single day is not the "be-all, end-all" for their human lives.

Connecting with students goes beyond knowing their name and being nice. It also means taking an active interest in their lives, conversing with them before and after class, demonstrating to them that you too are human and subject to the foibles of life, AND doing some of that within the lecture period. I incorporate personal stories analogous to my lecture topic so that they understand I am not simply some egg-headed professor, but a genuine human being. In doing so, not only have I connected to them, but they feel connected to me. They appreciate that I have children and that they are important. They begin to see me as not only a professor sharing my wisdom on a particular topic, but a role model worthy of emulation. I also use humor in the classroom. Humor breaks tension, demonstrates that I am human, and also invigorates the classroom and the learning process.

Connections with the Material

This is, perhaps, one of the most misunderstood elements in good teaching. As scholars, we almost always assume that any individual taking a course must have an explicit interest in the course. Wrong. Students take courses for a whole variety of reasons, including degree requirements, class availability, advisor recommendation, and boyfriends and girlfriends already enrolled in the course. I always think it's safe to assume that there is a small minority who are actually excited about the course material, but given most students' reticence about history, even that might be a stretch. As a result, it becomes my obligation to not only connect with the students, but foster a connection between the students and the material. I can do this through several means. First and foremost, I have to make sure that students understand the material. But then, I need to make sure that they understand in a deeper way by making sure they comprehend the relevance of the subject matter. For example, when I lectur e on "Reconstruction" (that historical period between 1865 and 1876 whereby the nation is trying to forge new bonds of union on the heels of the Civil War and include the newly freed slaves as part of that citizenry), I challenge my students to think about what they know of the modern Civil Rights movement, what they think about race as an issue today, and I ask whether slavery really ended. I then challenge my students to consider the reality of human trafficking, the fact that there are more slaves in the world today than in the 19th century and that 20,000 of them are enslaved in the United States. I challenge my students to ask themselves what they have done to perpetuate racism, stand up against racism, or have they simply been apathetic observers to what they universally regard as "evil." I connect my students to the material by making them active agents in historical change rather than simple observers of our dusty archaic past.

Connections with the material can also be made through alternative assignments. Let me be clear here, I am not a huge advocate of grade school assignments of workbook sheets, cut out hand Turkeys, or Pilgrim hat making. In fact, as most of my students will attest, I am a no-nonsense instructor. I rarely use powerpoint and when I do, I use it only for maps and illustrations. Powerpoint lecture notes are simply crutches for bad teaching. Instead, I ask my students to engage in a variety of activities beyond the four walls of the traditional classroom. I have them do community service projects (highlighting the power of grassroots democracy), special trips to historical sites, and community history projects (highlighting the role and importance of their own communities).

Process of Assignments as Instruction

This is another oft misunderstood element. If one carefully crafts one's course in the beginning, there will be ample opportunity to assess a student's comprehension of the material, their initiative in learning, and any advancements they made over the course of the class. Assignments are often viewed by instructors as instruments to measure a student's abilities. Yet, they often do not teach what the students will be graded upon. For example, a student may be asked to write an essay on some obscure historical subject and their subsequent essay may be rich with historical fact and evidence. But, because they have received little to no instruction on writing (in that history class or their English 101 class), the student may fail the assignment. This is patently unfair. We ought to be grading them on what WE instructed them. As a result, I see my assignments in a variety of ways. First, I regard my assignments as an opportunity for the student to learn what I want and expect from them. I am less concerned with the numerical grade I have given their work as I am with the student examining my comments, learning from those mistakes, and then improving upon them in their subsequent essays. In short, assignments serve as a gauge to where my students are and inform me of their status as writers so that I can truly help them to the next stage in their development. Later, I can look at those numerical scores in a much more traditional way, but assess them with an eye toward growth, improvement, and effort. A student who works to improve their writing will always receive an additional edge even if they are points away from the next score. A student with an 89% B+ might be advanced to an A grade if they have demonstrated effort, improvement, and a commitment to the class' welfare. Likewise, a student who has not made the effort, has declined assistance for improvement, and disrespects the opportunity offered them will not receive that same edge. They might have a 69.99999 D+++ and that will be the grade they ultimately receive. All assignments must, in my opinion, have a pedagogical goal apart from assessment.

Empowerment

The typical traditional student entering college has very little life experience where they were in charge and even few had any significant responsibilities. Four years later we expect these same students to enter the work force, be mature and responsible adults, and make all the right decisions. Yet, we rarely offer them real opportunities for taking command of their own lives let alone taking command of the material, subject, and the calls to action that accompany being a history major or any other socially-conscientious major. I believe, therefore, that its critical to offer students those type sof opportunities in a variety of ways.

First, by treating them like adults and informing them of the contractual nature of the class (as indicated in the syllabus), we informally educate them and give them a chance to act like an adult. If there are clear consequences spelled out, they will learn the rules of engagement. This was not always true at home or at high school for these students before their arrival at college. Mom and dad (if they were not divorced) always loved them, welcomed them home after a mistake was made, and often continued to enable the irresponsible behavior. High schools, as we all know, have long tolerated, accepted, and enabled poor decision-making by students. They were spoon-fed material, given low quality exams, and then forwarded on to the next grade. I let them know early, I will help them master the material, but their final score is THEIR final score. If anyone gets a good grade in my class it's because they earned it. Likewise, if anyone earned a poor score in my class, then they really earned it.

But empowerment also goes beyond simple lessons in maturity and responsibility. I call my students to action. I want them to be engaged citizens of the United States and engaged citizens of the world. I challenge them in class lectures to re-think all that they have been previously taught. I ask them to question the paradigms that the modern media machine has created for us. I ask them to question authority (even my own) and to take action against injustice. I make these challenges in the context of the traditional lecture, but I also give students an opportunity to be that "radical." Now, let's be clear, I do NOT impose my political beliefs or any party's dogma and doctrine onto my students. I do, however, make universal challenges regarding racism, sexism, and so on. As part of my classes, I typically require 1-2 community service oriented requirements.

They may range from raking leaves of senior citizens on the community each fall (what we call Random Acts of Kindness in Edinboro—RAKE) to creating an art piece that commemorates the work, wisdom, and life of Dr. Martin Luther King, Jr. They may be asked to participate in a rally, attend special lectures on the environment, or lead their own campaign for Human Trafficking awareness. All of the challenges are explicitly tied to the course material, but it allows the student to "take action," and do something beyond the four walls of the traditional classroom. In doing so, it makes them part of that world.

Empowerment for students also means representing their interests, supporting them in their struggles against university bureaucracy, a belligerent instructor, or apathetic employer. I am often called to not only write letters of recommendation for students applying to graduate programs, but also their efforts to become resident assistants and other campus positions. I am frequently asked for advice and I freely give it. I need to let the student know that they can solve their own problems, but that I can help them, guide them, and be a support when they struggle. It seems completely irrational when I hear my colleagues trash students who didn't follow this procedure or didn't handle the issue the way they ought to have. Who taught them the correct way? If no one has stepped forward and made an effort to assist our students develop the necessary skills for problem management, who will?

Fun, Pleasure, Laughter and Enjoyment

Lastly, classes need to be fun. Now don't get me wrong, I'm not suggesting we turn classes into circuses with clown cars and animal tricks. I am suggesting that learning can be fun, is fun, and has been fun for many of us for many years. The challenge here is to make it entertaining and fun enough such that the student begins to appreciate the subject, come to class, and then begin to see the value and rewards of simply knowing. I think the fact that my classes are routinely filled to capacity despite being held at 8am is testimony to this principle.

Moreover, my students (on average) complete more work than most classes of an equivalent level. For example, I teach a U.S. History II course that covers US History from 1865 to the present. It's a 200-level course. I require a 4-page autobiography, three essay exams, three 4-5 page papers based on the assigned monographs, 30 quizzes on the main text, a community service project, an art project, and mandatory attendance at the university's freshman common hour events. Students also have the opportunity for extra credit special lectures and events. In short, they are doing a lot of work. Yet, they continue to enroll and they stay in the class and they attend the 8am class period. They do it because class is fun.

How does one make a class fun? I'm sure certain classes are more conducive to that than others and there are certainly going to be some personalities in academia who simply cannot pull this off. In short, use your sense of humor. Tell stories, use funny accents, make the course material dynamic and challenging. Turn the class into periodic competitions, reward great behavior (those studying and prepared) and gently remind those who are not prepared.

Because experiences (and therefore lessons) are better remembered when attached to a positive emotion, it behooves us as instructors to make that experience rich with positive feelings. I had the opportunity many years ago now to hear Prof. James Zull speak. Zull was a biologist by training, but had also become one of the better teachers on the campus of Case Western University. He was invited to my campus to talk about teaching and the science of the brain behind "good" teaching. "Teachers who convey deeper meaning by their power of expression, both semantic and prosodic," he said " have a better chance to reach their students." Be human, be positive, and reach out to students and they WILL learn.

BUT, here's where it gets funky. Those seven topics that I just highlighted for the effective teaching of history are not just for the discipline of history. And in the end, strangely enough, it's really not about "teaching" at all. It's about "learning."

Students learn when those techniques are applied because the mind works along a similar fashion. It's like a lawn mower cutting grass. You'd never expect a lawn mower to filter your pool, vacuum your rug, or shave your legs. Yet, we often employ tools in the classroom in that same fashion. Some professors stand in front of a group of 18 to 22 year olds, read from their notes in a monotone voice ("Buehler? Buehler?") and expect the students to somehow absorb their wisdom. And, believe me, I get it. There are days where that seems like a tempting way to go about business. Likewise, I also appreciate that students need to be prepared for the real world and that they may not always have a passionate, engaged and thoughtful boss so they might need to experience that now and learn coping skills. But, I am not sure we, in academia, want to be the folks who do that, particularly given the anti-intellectualism in our nation. They will have plenty of time to discover and learn how to cope with the uninspired.

So, the way we teach ought to be more creatively designed in accordance with the way the student learns. That means, of course, we need to understand how they learn and what tools they are using to accomplish that learning. And, ta-dah, the tool that every student uses to learn is the human brain. As I have already alluded to at the beginning of this section, the seven techniques of good teaching I listed and briefly described are effective because that's exactly how the brain works. The brain is 1) organized and likes organization; 2) tailored to a world-view and set of experiences that requires us to know that specific audience; 3) woven together in a network of connections; 4) enjoys new material (or thoughts and memories) and stores it differently than older material (thoughts and memories); 5) is a processing machine that ultimately stores information in a variety of ways; 6) seeks to function in the most effective way for the user (the owner of that brain); and 7) likes pleasure. We will address this more when we get to the sections on memory, but I hope I have planted a seed in your brain so that when we do return to it, the connection will be stronger and richer.

Teaching History

Once an educator is clear on those basic elements, they can (at least for history) begin honing those skills and developing specialized skills for the discipline of history. These specific "history teaching tips" include: Definitions, Analogies, Accents, Activism, Visuals, and Relevance. I will refer to these as the Secondary-6.

Definitions

No student can be successful without the most fundamental definition of the topic they're addressing. We often forget that students come to us as nearly "blank slates" and that it is our obligation to help those students get to the next level. That transition, however, requires us to provide them with a basic definition of the assigned topic. For example, I lecture on "Reconstruction" every semester. I begin that lecture with an informal discussion of what "reconstruction" was and means. I let them offer up some inaccurate definitions and then weave them back to a discussion of the Civil War and the notion of Union, unity, and the new fabric of the American public. Inevitably, we together hammer out a solid definition of this historical time period. Of course, I will challenge them as to whether "reconstruction" was a success or a failure. I challenge them to ask whether the Civil War really ended or if slavery really was abolished. In short, students cannot understand the complexity of a topic without first having mastery of the most simple, rudimentary definition of the topic. I prefer to construct my buildings from ground up.

Analogies

I am not the best storyteller. I cannot even tell a joke of any great length. But, I try and I learn from the masters. What made Jesus a great storyteller and what made Abraham Lincoln a great storyteller all emerge from their fundamental skill and developing an analogy within a story. Whether it's a full-blown allegory or a simple analogy embedded into the larger story, those two men were capable of capturing an audience's attention and educate them on a larger topic. They did it through analogies.

There are several reasons why analogies are effective. First, it is a side-story that reduces a complex nuanced story into a simple, memorable little case study. Second, the parallel story used reinforces the memory of the first. It's simply a second way of telling the same story and that second version only compliments the first. When we get to memory in this book, we will see that repetition is a valuable tool for memory and thinking in general. The analogy is typically an alternative and more creative way of telling that story. It's a portion that can entertain the viewer as well as educate. Lastly, the analogy allows the storyteller to insert personal, relate-able information that will further the bonds between the professor and the student.

Here's an example I often use in my World War I and World War II lectures. In those lectures I have introduced and defined the term "geopolitics" and have asked the students to think how geography might have affected Germany's strategy during these two important wars. Naturally, students can see the map and they quickly realize that Germany is surrounded by its enemies. I then ask them what might there strategy be. Before they can offer wrong answers, I quickly set up a model in class. In the front row, I identify three students seated side-by-side and I identify the one in the middle as the German nation and the students to each side as France and Russia/Soviet Union (depending on the war). But rather than being in a struggle for the continent, I propose that they are in bar room brawl. How does one eliminate one opponent standing next to them while another enemy is drinking a beer to their rear. I advise them, it should be noted, that I do not condone bar room brawls or any form of violence. I then walk them through Germany's strategy. In WWI, they will launch a lightning-like strike across Belgium in order to disable the French. The Schlieffen Plan was born out of European geopolitics. In WWII, I remind them that the Schlieffen Plan was not as effective as they had hoped and ask them now what would they do. I then teach them, through the same trio of students, that maybe a more effective way of taking over Europe, under those geopolitical circumstances, might be to sign a Non-Aggression Pact with the Soviets and then launch that lightning-like strike (blitzkrieg) into France. In doing so, the Germans were able to neutralize one foe, attack the second, and then once completed, turn their attention back to the original enemy and invade the Soviet Union. This was all done as a series of analogies—using the bar room struggle and the model of students at the front of the class. Now, this works and students remember it because I have taken a complex diplomatic and military story and consolidated into a memorable bar room analogy. It's also effective because I have unsuspectingly reinforced their memory of the real story with an analogous one. Lastly, the story breaks the pace, makes it seem more hands-on history and reveals to the students (whether that's a good thing or not) that I have been in bars and witnessed bar room brawls. Although I will have to admit, I was not much of a brawler myself. At El Vaqueros in Helena, Montana, I witnessed (some say initiated) a bar room brawl that cleared the entire place with the exception of me. While all the patrons and employees were outside puffing up their chests and awaiting blood to spill, I was safely inside the bar where I slipped behind the counter, filled pitcher after pitcher of beer and began filling every patrons' glass with the beer of my choice. Lesson learned: bar room brawls can be fun and they make great classroom analogies.

The greatest classroom analogy, for which most of my students have been sworn to secrecy, is my "cheaters" analogy during my Cold War lecture. In short, this lecture always follows a mid-term examination. Students are typically anxious about their scores and are eager to have their tests returned. When I enter class that day, however, I promptly put the key words and terms for the Cold War on the board and then take a seat where I refrain making any eye contact with the students. I go so far as to pout and scowl hoping to give students the impression that I am mad or upset about something. Then, as class begins, I rise and pause. Because of my own nerves regarding this theatrical production, I begin to shake. I spend approximately ten minutes revealing to them that I have been told by a handful of their classmates that there was widespread cheating on the last exam. I tell them how disappointed I am, how hurt I am because I am so friendly and flexible with them. I tell them I feel betrayed and I tell them, consistently, that they know who cheated and they know it's grounds for expulsion. After a ten minute accusation period, I tell them that I have spoken with the Dean and my department chair and the only solution that seems reasonable is for every student to write either a confession where they admit their guilt or a letter indicating what they know and who they saw cheating. The class is silent. Students are practically bug-eyed in shock. I then slowly confess that the entire matter was fabricated and that I wanted them to feel the fear, paranoia, sense of false charges that permeated the Cold War era and the days of McCarthyism. From there, after more de-briefing (including a reiteration that I really do NOT want letters from them and a promise that they won't tell their classmates), I lecture on the Cold war and McCarthyism. Throughout that lecture, I deliberately confuse "communist" and "cheater" to strengthen the analogy of false accusations. Dozens of former students have later confessed that they use the same technique successfully in their own high school classrooms. It may be unorthodox, but they remembered the material.

Accents

This task is a bit harder for some and I do not recommend it for every class or every lecture. The important lesson is to interject humor and fun into your course material in any way possible. I do this through the use of stereotypic accents representing the different cultures and ethnicities represented in American society. In each case, however, I note for the students that my stereotyping is not an accurate portrayal of the people as a whole. In my lectures on "Industrialization" I use an Italian-American accent to highlight the abuse of the American worker, Henry Ford's use of a worker to speed up the assembly line (what was called the "gallopini"). In my lectures on WWII and the Cold War, I drag out German and Russian accents and highlight for the student how those portrayals minimize our planet neighbors and warp and distort our sense of American "exceptionalism." All the while, however, the student finds the lecture memorable and educational. To this day, I have former students approach me on the street and tell me they have not forgotten my lecture on WWI and the "Schlieffen Plan" (which, of course, I and they always say in a thick German accent). Any means by which to make the course memorable is a valuable class tool.

As James Zull notes, "teachers who convey deeper meaning by their power of expression, both semantic and prosodic, have a better chance to reach their students." This means that the old monotone professor, void of facial expressions who only uses mundane words and phrases will not likely reach their students. There is a reason, after all, poetry and drama have survived after all these years.

Now this seems like a cheap gimmick. Maybe it is. BUT, what it actually does is create an alternate personality. It may make the student laugh, but it allows them to see that the story involves "others."

Activism

Students need to be engaged. They need to be engaged with the material and the instructor, but they also need to be engaged with the world. They need to be able to actively convert the lessons they learned in class to the world in which they live. In doing so, they not only learn the relevance of the material, but also learn they have not only the power to change the world, but an obligation to serve that world.

Apathy, as a social disease, is in my opinion largely responsible for today's social ills. Part of that apathy is born out of the worlds' complexity. Students simply do not understand what is happening around them, nor do they know necessarily how to educate themselves about that world. Some might argue that the answers to all of the world's questions can now be answered with a few quick taps of the finger on the computer keyboard. Yet, it is that very internet that is making the world so baffling for some. There are too many answers, too many dubious responses and no clear way to determine which is correct. Our students may be literate, but that only applies to the written word. Our students (and many of our colleagues) are simply information illiterate. Students are also apathetic out of sheer affluence. Why would an upper-class American male necessarily care about something that doesn't affect him?

Why would a teenage girl care about anything other than finding her own place and success in American society? Well, we know the answers. But, how do we convey that to our students and empower them to make that change.

Giving "activism" exercises forces them to find reliable information and act upon it. When I ask students if slavery really ended in 1865 with the passage of the 13th Amendment, we have a lengthy discussion about slavery, slavery in the South after 1865 (sharecropping, crop-lien systems, chain gangs, and the like); and then continue to address the topic of modern slavery in the United States. I ask them how slavery might be different today given that there are 20,000 slaves in the US and over 20 million worldwide. I then challenge students to take the next step and develop a project associated with their new historically-based findings. They have, as a result, held conferences, developed K-12 curriculum, staffed awareness tables and panels, coordinated awareness walks through the community and created local websites to spread the information. In doing so, these American students took an active role in improving society, seen the rewards of their work, and shaken that mantle of apathy.

I'm not necessarily interested in them becoming radicals of any flavor, but I want them to realize that a democracy takes work; it requires an active citizen population who understand the forces at play in their nation and who vote and serve their communities in an active vibrant way.

Visuals

Any good education major will tell you that one of the first things they learn is that every student has a different learning style. They can name the different styles—from auditory learner to a visual learner to a kinetic learner to combinations and so on and so on. I believe this to be true, but I also understand that students also need to learn other styles and need to be exposed to other styles over the course of their education. They will, after all, enter a workforce where their employer will probably NOT be familiar with these styles. Nonetheless, I try to incorporate as mean different teaching approaches into my lectures as possible. I change my auditory approach with both the inflection and pace and (as noted earlier) through silly accents. I also offer a small dose of visual aids. I use maps when appropriate and when my classroom is equipped with modern technology I also use art and illustrations. I do NOT use powerpoint for my lecture notes. That' s simply sloppy teaching. If I wanted them to just re-read my lecture notes without commentary, I would have had them printed off and we could have saved valuable time for everyone involved. The visual aids are designed to supplement instruction, allow an additional memory connection between the subject matter and the students' existing memory base.

Relevance

Lastly, students need to know why the course material is relevant. They need to know why that particular historical example is worth remembering. It's not good enough to simply say "Because!" or "you need to know where you came from." Students want to know in what ways can that information be used.

So, before each lecture and at the conclusion of each lecture, I reiterate exactly WHY that lecture has relevance in a 20-year old students' life. The answers may range from the value of a 3rd party politics and their understanding of current election contests to the behavior of nations in war.

Now, this has been traditionally the most difficult element for historians to do with students. We have hesitated in trying to tell students "why" they needed to know it and how it applied, but hoped that they would see that, of course, it's relevant, important, and applicable. We hoped that the material somehow sold itself. But, students didn't see it. How could they? They had Mrs. McGillicuddy and Coach Schmucker as their teachers.

This process of "making relevance" is known as "emplotment" and "reemplotment." In short, we continuously make connections between events and thereby apply meaning to both those past events as well as present ones. If a student cannot be actively encouraged to do so, then we have failed as teachers. It's only those connections, after all, that will foster greater critical thinking.

As was the case for the first seven general techniques, these additional six skills for the classroom bear the same power. They are not just "teaching" tricks, but are proven ways in which students learn. And, as I have already suggested with the Ultra-7, these factors for the classroom also adhere to the structure and function of the brain. In short, the brain: 1) employs definitions and seeks out definitions for the world around it; 2) seeks parallels between the defined things in the world for a more complex understanding of that world; 3)

appreciates differences, like accents, to distinguish between the

complex parts; 4) seeks to integrate itself into the functioning of

the world through "activism" and other means; 5) engages in all

of these discernment processes through the senses, namely

through sight; and 6) wants to know why information is relevant

to their newly-prescribed world. So, again, we ought to be

teaching to facilitate learning. We ought not expect that

learning will necessarily be the by-product of what we do in the

classroom. Instead, we ought to tailor our classroom skills

according to the known ways in which the human brain (and,

therefore, memory) operates.

CHAPTER SEVEN

Tricks of the Memory Trade, the Human Brain, and Other Exposed Parts

Now, because we know the brain is malleable, we can make the next step and that is argue that there are multiple ways to manipulate the brain such that it remembers what we want it to remember. I'll remind the reader here that the brain, like sports or music, requires practice. If we are to expect it to remember more than what will simply allow us to survive, we have to employ some tricks to help us remember. In short, we will develop new channels or networks that will facilitate greater memory. I will also note here that the more one practices the art of memory, the better they will become at remembering new things. For example, I have long been able to remember the first one hundred winners of the Kentucky Derby. My mind created channels and "learned" those horses named at the same time how memory channels were made. In doing so, subsequent efforts at rote memorization (whether it be lists of royalty or winners of the Superbowl) became significantly easier.

Our goal is not to make you into a freak-show exhibit or the subject a motion picture, like Kim Peek, but to provide you with better tools to remember and thereby think and thereby survive. Kim Peek, by the way, had a prodigious memory. He could read two pages from different books simultaneously and remember both pages forever. He would serve as a partial inspiration for Dustin Hoffman's character in Rain Man.

So, let's see some of the ways in which the mind (or at least mine) has organized information in a memorable way. They are, in no particular order: linking, visualization, muscle-memory, rhyming, repeating, writing, acronyms, reduction patterns, storytime, and dreams.

Links

This is, in my mind, the easiest memory trick to employ, but if overused can also be the most debilitating. In short, as you are asked to remember something form a link between the item to be memorized and something else that will trigger that memory. For example, in one of my earliest courses I had a student whose last name was shared by that of an animal. Naturally, I linked the woman's name to that animal. I also link students' names to the clothes they wore that first day, my first impression of them, a rock group, or an ethnic identity. A student named Vinny Piccolino, for example, was easy to remember because he not only looked Italian, but I conjured an image of him working for the mob. He was, in my memory, not simply a good student who worked hard, but Vinny "The Godfather" Piccolino. In effect, what our brain is doing when we form links is strengthening axonic connections and multiplying the number of axon connections to that particular synaptic connection. The greater the number of connections (or links) means that the synaptic connection grows stronger and is more likely to be remembered. In short, we have helped create a series of "feedback loops." Let's remind ourselves what Eric Kandel wrote and what we quoted from him in the previous chapter: "To be useful," he said, "a memory has to be recalled. Memory retrieval depends on the presence of appropriate cues that an animal can associate with its learning experience." Let us further remind ourselves, that making connections between events is what allows us to apply meaning to both past and present events. Again, we must make connections. And remember, just in the previous chapter I identified how just about all information technology was designed to serve as a memory tool. Computers today are memory tools and the reason I am bringing them up now is that within most websites and computer information records, we find connections being made between ideas. We have been smart enough to realize what they are and we call them "links." We have links between websites and such, but we also create within our own heads "links" that allow us to better manage, retain, and recall stored memories. But, again, it's all about connections.

Visualize

Visualization is really just a sub-category of linkages. With this trick, you as a "rememberer" are asked to form visual connections to the memory subject. This visual connection may be an artificially constructed image. For example, a student named Peter Smith may look like a lion and so I envision the lion, Peter, and pair them in my memory. Or, I may remember a student purely through the visual context in which I first met them. I met a student with the last of Statz next to a U.S. map. I immediately associated the student with the states I could see behind him. This was a product of where I met the student, but helped me remember their name every day in class. It is worth noting that this type of situational memory can backfire when you are unexpectedly confronted by the student outside the four walls of the regular classroom. Knowing that you may have to do some spatial juggling, however, can partially resolve this dilemma.

This visualization trick can be done on the spot or with greater reflection. I recommend both. Take a few seconds to mentally visualize a connection, put the name to the face, and, in doing so, you have kept the memory alive a little bit longer and hopefully it can be consolidated to long-term memory. This idea of reflection is also of great value. It not only requires more time and thereby induces long-term memorization, but it allows for greater detail of that memory to be absorbed. Just as meditative practices can involve an "incremental reprogramming" of the mind, simple reflection can allow incremental reconnecting of that memory to other memories.

We know that this trick works as many of the great memory trick artists use this practice. S. V. Sherashevsky entertained audiences all across the Soviet Union in the 1930s with a grand display of his memory skills. Those who have subsequently studied Sherashevsky suggest that he may have had "synesthesia" or an acute sensory perception. It worked for Sherashevsky and it can work for you (perhaps not so brilliantly) if you just practice.

Visualization also works because it allows our brains to make certain connections, foster a deeper and richer understanding and interpretation of that memory. It's almost like meditation. If you have ever attended a yoga session or seen them being done on TV, you'll recognize the familiar request of the yoga instructor "to visualize yourself" or "visualize this" or "visualize that." Meditation and the visualization process allows for "incremental reprogramming" of the mind. If our task is to remember and re-program then certainly this may be a useful tool.

Muscle-Memory

Everyone has heard of "muscle-memory" on one fashion or another. This is also referred to as unconscious memory or implicit memory. It is a deeply embedded memory that hinge son the procedure being completed. It is simply the concept that if one routinely practices a physical act (from typing to skiing to football), the participant involved will experience muscle memory. In short, the internal body memory has been so engrained that there is little conscious effort to recall the desired act. Sheer repetition has trained the body to repeat the physical act under parallel circumstances. This idea reinforces the idea that practice and training are effective memory tools. But, it also suggests that memory can have a physical component. I rarely employ this when trying to recall students' names. But, I have found it useful on other areas, like typing. I have never taken a typing class in my life (and, frankly, it shows). I have, however, poked and pegged my way through three books, countless articles and the like to generally know the area in which my finger s are supposed to go. Unless, of course, the word is "beautiful" for which some reason my mind can never grasp and cannot type at the same lightning-like speed I do all other words. That being said, the point here is that our physical body is not divorced from our brain and we can use that body to help us remember. For some of you, you may find it particularly useful to walk, pace, or engage in some activity to stimulate memory. I know several students who tell me that the tapping of their pencils or pens helps them jumpstart certain memory patterns. If it works, do it: Move and memorize.

Rhyme

Have you ever noticed that children can repeat complex song lyrics, but can't remember their assigned chores? Or they can repeat a lengthy children's rhyme but they cannot repeat the name s of Presidents or states? In large part, I believe, this is because the mind is accustomed to arranging things in patterns. We, as a species, have that mental advantage—we can see patterns. Remember when your kindergarten teacher was teaching you shapes and patterns? She'd say "square, circle, square, circle—what comes next?" And, of course, we all giggled at the ridiculously easy question and screamed out "SQUARE!" (except for little Jimmy Smolina who wasn't paying attention anyway). That pattern of assigning patterns and putting it to a tune enables some individuals to better remember things. One of my favorite is the mnemonic tune to assist British kids memorize their British Kings and Queens. It goes like this:

Willy, Willy, Harry, Ste,

Harry, Dick, John, Harry three,

One, two, three Neds, Richard two,

Henries four, five, six – then who?

Edwards four, five, Dick the bad,

Harries twain and Ned the lad,

Mary, Bessie, James the vain,

Charlie, Charlie, James again,

William & Mary, Anna Gloria,

Four Georges, William and Victoria,

Edward, George, then Ned the eighth

quickly goes and abdicat'th,

leaving George, then Liz the second,

and with Charlie next it's reckoned.

That simple seven stanza poem allows British kids to remember their past Kings and Queens and cover nearly 1000 years of history. Rhyming is one of the most culturally universal mnemonic devices. Rhyming was such a common way of teaching and embedding history in the 19th century, that writer and humorist Mark Twain once wrote that "history doesn't repeat itself, but it rhymes."

Repeat

The brain is like a muscle. With greater use, the brain gets stronger. This is not a hard thing to understand. Unfortunately, many students (young and old alike) are not willing to put in the time necessary for this trick. Most people trying to employ improved memory techniques are simply looking for a quick remedy to a temporary crisis, namely an impending exam. This trick, while involving a commitment of time, has the best long-term results. In short, repeat the desired information and then repeat again. The more the items are repeated, the stronger the synaptic bonds are within the mental circuitry.

As a college student, after requisite hours of traditional studying, I took the last few hours of my test preparation to commit to memory my outline for my thesis and the supporting evidence I planned to use. I did this outline memorization by repeating over and over the basic elements until they were so well-engrained that they rolled off my tongue as easy as my own name. This repetition process is what neuroscientists and psychologists have referred to as "rehearsal systems." The repetition of the fact (say, your new girlfriend's phone number) allows the memory to "stay alive" long enough for the brain to remember it. It stays at the forefront of the mind such that a "sensory buffer" can be it so may be implemented around it. Or, in other words, by repeating so many times that the axon shaft and the synaptic connections are so strengthened and so robust that they cannot be easily broken. This repetition is also instrumental in shifting the memory from explicit memory to implicit memory.

Maurice Halbwachs, one of the first great thinkers about collective memory, noted that while memories are often "selective," that personal memories also fade without repetition. Certain memories we have about our childhood have only persisted because our mothers told us those stories repeatedly. Those same mothers, now as grandmothers, continued to re-tell the story (whether it was true or not) to our children. The memory persisted because it was repeated and it was repeated often. How many of us have heard our favorite uncle tell this story or that story so many times that we ourselves could tell it as adeptly as he does? That's the power of repetition. But note, there is a certain danger here. For as we continue to repeat our uncle's legendary war story or the shaman repeats the ancient creation myth, we tend to inadvertently include details that were not part of the original.

In doing so, we create what Halbwachs calls the "imago" or idealized image.

If one repeats information out loud, they are also actively engaging other areas of the brain as reinforcers for the memory. This verbal rehearsal creates, in effect, a "phonological loop" that employs simple memory rehearsal tricks, but adds the value of the spoken and heard word. Constant repetition can convert explicit memories to implicit ones. That is the goal, after all, to be able to easily recall anything rather than have it dangle unwittingly from the tip of our tongue.

Write

While repetition reinforces memories, the repeated writing of desired elements will reinforce the memory even more. The literal act of writing is a repetition of the desired memory, but it also employs the physical nature of remembering. It is, in effect, a combination of both the muscle-memory technique as well as repetition. But, the best thing about this whole trick is that it can easily be reduced. If one were to write one's entire class notes for my class, the first re-write might take up 40 or so pages. But, the second re-write of those notes will be quickly reduced to 20 pages. This will occur in part because the notetaker will do two things: 1) omit things unnecessary for the memorization of the specific event or story; and 2) consolidate information or reduce the information to a manageable amount. By the time one re-writes the notes a third and fourth time, the notes can be reduced even further. When I was a college punk, I could reduce hundreds of pages of notes down to a one page outline of all the important sub-topics and thesis arguments.

In the 19th century and even into the early 20th century, many educators emphasized the use of rote memorization. They did this to teach oratory skills to the students, but it had many hidden benefits. Not only did the students become skilled speakers, but the practice and effort involved in that rote memorization often included them writing and re-writing the subject matter. This improved their handwriting, fostered better memory skills, and gave them a strong neuronal network with which to associate future memories. To this day, I still recite Rudyard Kipling. Thank you, Mrs. Williams!

Acronyms

Another useful memory tool is the use of acronyms. Many of you are already familiar with this mnemonic device on one way or another. Many of you may have already used it in life. The acronym HOMES, for example, is a popular one. HOMES is the acronym that allows us to remember the name sof the 5 Great Lakes: Huron, Ontario, Michigan, Erie, and Superior. But this mnemonic trick is very simple and effective. And, by the way, they need not spell out real words. You could, if you so desired, use WAJM as a cue to remember the first four

President so the United States: Washington, Adams, Jefferson, and Madison. And, because they are simply cues, they still require the student to learn the "real" names. In high school, I used an elaborate acronym to remember my "etre" verbs. The acronym was DR. MRS. VANDERTRAMP. The verbs are: descendre, redescendre, monter, remonter, sortir, venir, arriver, naitre, devenir, entrer, rentrer, mourir, and partir and passer. Each letter served as a cue for the special verb conjugations in past tense that required "etre." Yet, as you might be able to guess by the length of that acronym even "DR. Mrs. VANDERTRAMP" could not always bail me out of a French test. As a result, I employed a complimentary mnemonic device and that was to remember that almost all of the verbs I needed to remember had a relationship to a house. The terms could be remembered that way too. They are arriver (to arrive...at the house), descendre (to descend / go downstairs...in the house); redescendre (to descend again), entrer (to enter), rentrer (to re-enter), monter (to climb), remonter (to climb again), mourir (to die), naître (to be born)...and so on.

The use of acronyms seems particularly useful when trying to memorize something at the last minute and where the situation may not require great depth in understanding.

Reduce

Another useful trick is to reduce what is required to be known into small digestible parts. It's actually very simple. In short, it is much harder to remember 100 items than it is to remember 20 groups of five items. Our minds simply prefer smaller packages. Moreover, once your mind has mastered the first 10 units, it can focus its attention on the remaining items to be memorized. This technique will be more readily examined and demonstrated in a moment when we take an in-depth analytical look at my memory of the Kentucky Derby winners. But some hints for this trick include finding internal patterns, arrange according to a system (alphabet, chronology), and look for transitions between the reduced groups.

Storytime

We have all grown up hearing stories---from Little Red Riding
Hood to the Three Little Pigs. The origins of many of those
stories were to teach children certain lessons. Some, like
Hansel and Gretel, were stories devised to warn us about
threats in society...whether it was old women (witches) or
wolves in the woods. Stories are effective tools for teaching
because they entertain, have vivid detailed elements, and
because the story was simple and could be easily re-told. All
educational lessons ought to fit that criteria. Stories are also
effective because they play into our existing memories.

As Eric Kandel has further noted, "For a memory to persist, the
incoming information must be thoroughly and deeply
processed. This is accomplished by attending to the
information and associating it meaningful and systematically
with knowledge already well established in memory." This

means that we simply have to make a series of associations, but ones that already are remembered.

Dream

I slipped this one in here for several reasons. First, I believe a good night's rest is critical to our ability to do well under any circumstance. Sleep, and the dreams that come with it, also serve as our brain's opportunity to digest information, process it, circulate it and make deeper connections, and then aid us in our retention and recall of those memories. Dreams, as we will later see, are also critical to our imagination and fears. As a young master's student at UCLA, I took an intensive summer Chinese language program. I took the class for hours in the morning and sat in the foreign language lab well into the late afternoon every day. At night I studied and practiced m characters. I was a good student. But, on the eve of my final exam, I was gripped with fear. When I slept that night, I dreamt entirely in Chinese. When I awoke, my fears had subsided and I promptly went to class and aced my final exam. Dreams, as evident in that case study, allowed me to address my fears, practice my language, and instill me with confidence that I was going to do well and that I had done all that was necessary.

The Kentucky Derby: An Example of Memory Control

This section is designed to offer specific example how multiple memory tricks can be employed for a larger body of information. It could have been used for much more valuable or important information, but I just happened to do it with the first 100 winners of the Kentucky Derby. So, let's look at them and how it works:

1875   Aristides

1876   Vagrant

1877   Baden Baden

1878   Day Star

1879   Lord Murphy

Now, this section is unique in that there were no memory tricks employed. Why? Well, that's because typically the beginning of large series gets so much exposure that the multiple repetition of it over and over serves to embed the memory of these five horses names fully into the rememberer's brain. But, note that the use of years (essential for this body of information) also serves as an anchor. It allows the individual to remember certain years. When I started looking at the glass upon which this information was etched, I automatically hooked onto several years—1889 in which the horse Spokane won (I was born in that great Pacific Northwest city) and 1965 in which the horse Lucky Debonair won (the year I was born). Over the course of the time I finished memorizing the list, I had made other connections that proved useful to triggering my memory for that specific horse.

1880   Fonso

1881   Hindoo

1882   Apollo

1883   Leonatus

1884   Buchanan

Now, for this section I employed several other

techniques. First, to make the transition from the first set, I

identified the connection between "Lord Murphy" (representing

royalty in my mind) to the theme these five horses seemed to

reflect :ancient or classical traditions. Note that Ancient

Hinduism, ancient Greek god Apollo and Roman leader

Leonatus' names are applied to 3 out of the 5 horses. In my

mind I stretched it a little further and conjured up a royal image

of Arthur Fonzarelli (Fonso) and President James Buchanan. The

use of royalty, Fonzi and an American President are all evidence

of memory made by connections. Thus, I knew from the "Lord

Murphy" reference that the next 5 were the royal 5. The order of these horses also fell quickly in line by sheer repetition.

1885   Joe Cotton

1886   Ben Ali

1887   Montrose

1888   Macbeth II

1889   Spokane

To transition to this set of five horses, I connected President Buchanan (1857-1861) and Joe Cotton. In my mind, this was a seamless transition as Buchanan served as our last president before the Civil War, failing miserably to appease or address the slavery issue. Of course, slavery occurred predominantly in the American South where "Cotton was King." From there, I connected slavery to a 20th century American hero who stood up against racism, Muhammad Ali and imagined that fiery and poetic boxer with a rose between his teeth. The alliteration of Montrose led me to Macbeth II and I had already embedded into my head that Spokane won the

1889 race. So, that set of five was now complete.

1890   Riley

1891   Kingman

1892   Azra

1893   Lookout

1894   Chant

1895   Halma

This section is also a unique section. I found that it was

easier to remember the latter sections of horses if they were

clumped into five year periods ending in five year increments at

"5" and "0." So, I added one additional horse to this section. As

you will see , it further facilitated other mnemonic devices. I

shifted from Spokane in 1889 to Riley in 1890 by imagining that

Riley was the name of an IWW worker arrested for his Free

Speech activities in the city of Spokane. Although that historical incident (The Spokane Free Speech Fight) was still 20 years

away when Spokane won, it worked in my head. The next 5

horses were remembered as an acronym KALCH. So, once the

Spokane-Riley transition was made, the next five rolled easily

off.

1896   Ben Brush

1897   Typhoon

1898   Plaudit

1899   Manuel

1900   Lt. Gibson

The 1895 winner of the Kentucky Derby was a horse

named Halma and the name conjured up the image of a woman

with luscious dark flowing hair. I was able to thus make the

transition to 1896 with the horse Ben Brush whose name stirred

images of a hairbrush going through Halma's dark mane. Of

course, Halma's hair needed a brushing because she had just

undergone a horrible windstorm that messed it up and so the

horse's name, Typhoon, was easy to recall. The next three

horse stood alone. I envisioned Plaudit as an award or a medal

for some award, Manuel was the Spanish officer receiving that

award (note that this in the heart of the Spanish-American War)

and the following year in 1900 an American won that award, Lt.

Gibson. So, here in these last three I have explicitly woven

together a story and used my previous understanding of the

history of that time period.

1901   His Eminence

1902   Alan-A-Dale

1903   Judge Himes

1904   Elwood

1905   Agile

1906   Sir Huon

1907   Pink Star

1908   Stone Street

1909   Wintergreen

1910   Donau

1911   Meridian

1912   Worth

1913   Donerail

1914   Old Rosebud

1915   Regret

1916   George Smith

1917   Omar Khayyam

1918   Exterminator

1919   Sir Barton

1920   Paul Jones

1921   Behave Yourself

1922   Morvich

1923   Zev

1924   Black Gold

1925   Flying Ebony

Ok, so now it appears upon the first read that this

section was some how-to guide for memory building and to a

certain degree it was. My intent, however, was not to reveal my secrets, expose my magical art to my students, or make a buck off some cheap snake-oil memory book. As was the case with the section on the teaching of history, both the Ultra-7 and the Secondary-6, these tricks are effective because that's how the brain works, that's how memory works, and that's how students can learn. So, it seems only logical that the memory tricks might, in fact, share some features with those "teaching" or "learning" skills.

So, let me briefly review the Ultra-7 and Secondary-6. The Ultra-7 techniques included organization, audience, connections, relationship to the material, the process of assignments, empowerment, and fun. The Secondary-6 techniques included definitions, analogies, accents, activism, visuals, and relevance. If you look closely, you will see some striking similarities between those features and the "tricks" listed for memory retrieval. Those memory retrieval tricks were: linking, visualization, muscle-memory, rhyming, repeating, writing, acronyms, reduction patterns, storytime, and dreams. You will note that the "trick" of "linking" is exactly what we called for in "connections" and "analogies." You will note that "trick" of "visualization" and "muscle-memory" is associated with "visuals" and the use of other senses. The chart below identifies a full list of the parallels, but I think you can see the point. Our brain memorizes things well when we use the brain as it was designed to be used. In thinking about it this way, we can begin to reassess the "education crisis" that so many folks moan about here in the United States. Perhaps the problem in our educational system is that we are simply not asking our children to use their brains in the most effective and optimal ways.

Memory   Teaching

Advanced Learning

Linking	Connections
Analogies	
Visualization	Material
Visuals	
Muscle-memory	Empowerment
Activism	
Rhyming	Material
Analogies	
Repeating	Process
Analogies	
Writing	Process
Accents	
Acronyms	Organization
Definitions	
Reduction patterns	Organization
Definitions	

Storytime   Audience

Relevance

Dreams   Fun

Relevance

I'm not sure I need to go into further description and analysis with regard to the parallels between memory, teaching, learning, and the brain. Suffice it to say, they are linked. As a result, it is not so far-fetched then to say that the sheer act of being requires a series of complicated mental processes all of which involve memory. Being is remembering.

But, both take time. Muller and Alfonse Pilzecker believed memory took time to fixate in the brain, or as they termed it "konsoliderung." This "consolidation" process is now much more complicated than scientists initially understood.

"For a memory to persist," Kandel writes, "the incoming information must be thoroughly and deeply processed. This is accomplished by attending to the information and associating it meaningful and systematically with knowledge already well established in memory." If that's the case the, the idea of foundational memory is critical. The more we can remember, the more we will be able to remember.

If that is the case, and that's exactly what I am suggesting here, then so too we must come to the conclusion that History is the process of being. It is the most human of disciplines because it IS what we do, it IS who we are, it is WHY we are.

CHAPTER EIGHT

Wrapping it All Up: The Conclusion

When a historian begins a research project, we typically begin with some question we want to answer. There is no hypothesis (or there shouldn't be) as we have yet to gather the evidence to know what that answer may even look like and we don't want to influence the conclusion by looking for what we presume to be the answer. Instead, we ask big sweeping questions. For example, for my book Engendered Death: Pennsylvania Women Who Kill, I began by examining one specific case—the Edna Mumbulo story in 1930. I wanted to know everything about the case. That research took me to court records, newspaper accounts, genealogical files, Church records, and family correspondence as well as a treasure trove of secondary literature about women who kill, the Great Depression, and Erie, Pennsylvania. We gather and gather and gather until we faithfully believe we have exhausted our topic. In my case, the project got so out of hand that I unilaterally placed parameters on the work and so I limited it to the state of

Pennsylvania. Once I collected all the material, I discovered that

the real story for me lay not in the motive or method for the

crimes, but in how society perceived and portrayed these

women. As a result, I had to explore the secondary literature on

gender, media, and the justice system. We, as historians, we

have a clear and systematic process by which we operate, but

our destinations are never clear. And we often end in

unexpected places.

In this work, I began with a clear and concise question:

what is the relationship between memory, history, and dreams?

My process and my question may have been clear, but where I

have ended up is beyond what I could have ever imagined. It

has launched me into a journey into not only memory, history,

and dreams, but teaching, learning, and the way our brain

operates. But, more importantly, it has brought me on a

journey of self-reflection and into an exorcism of my final dying

thoughts. I have written three books prior to this: Engendered

Death: Pennsylvania Women Who Kill (2011); Crime and

Punishment in Oregon, 1875-1915 (2008); and Invisible City:

Erie, Pennsylvania, 1930-1960s (2014). And I have three other

books beyond this waiting for a publisher. My writing has been

part of my discipline. It is my obligation. I have a duty as a

historian to give back to the body of literature; to contribute to

the body of knowledge and to preserve our memory of the past.

I am a guardian of the past and, as a result, I haunt that past. In

doing so, I have not only preserved part of that fading past and

memory, but I have preserved part of myself. My words (albeit

the stories of others) are me. One could, I suppose, decipher

who Joseph Laythe is by examining all my works and unraveling

from it my personal philosophies and values. This work,

however, has been significantly different. It has, from the

inception of the writing process, been infused with my story, my

impending death, and my reflections on the life I have been

blessed to live. And so, I haunt this work.

Re-Assessment

What is necessary to remember about this work will depend heavily upon what you, the reader, deem important at this point in your own venture. Some readers may come away from this book with tips on how to teach better. Some may be inspired to improve their memory and, in doing so, improve their brains. Others may be sparked to explore the ideas of dreams while others may find a renewed passion for history. Or, as I have found in the process of writing it, some may find a joy in the complexity and interconnectedness of life itself.

So many more questions are ultimately born out of this exercise than we actually answered. Like--What is necessary to Remember? (The student question "Do I need to remember this?" is mocked and ridiculed, but is a valuable question essential to human survival)

What is the Human Experience? Are digital artificial intelligence and intelligent-design making the need for human memory less relevant? If AI (or artificial intelligence) is close or equal to human experience where does dreaming come in and to what degree does it give us the "advantage" over the future?

In short, who are we? Who do we want to be?

History=Collective memories. Collective memories=an assemblage of individual memories. Individual memories=thoughts + experiences. Thoughts + Experiences= Dreams. Thoughts+ Experiences= History. Therefore, is it unreasonable to conclude that history=dreams. Are they not both a refashioning of the past in the mind of the observer? Are they not both a lens by which we can re-think ourselves and our planet? Are they not both just fragments of a complicated mind? What if?

What If History?

The discipline I teach has rarely been speculative. Many historians have scoffed at the idea of "what if" history or speculative history because, from their narrow-minded perspective, it offers little insight into what is and can only dream for what might have been or what might be. In short, it appears to them to not be very scientific. I'm suggesting here that speculative history or "what if" history is not only fun, but valuable.

When I was young in the 1970s, I remember watching Saturday Night Live. That late night sketch show had two "what if" skits that have been burned into my brain. The first was based on the premise of "What if Eleanor Roosevelt could fly?" The skit then showed the homely first lady leading a squadron of bombers in v-formation in a raid upon our World War Two enemies. As a small boy, I thought it was funny. As an adult college history professor, I have used that story to jumpstart discussions about Mrs. Roosevelt, women's roles in the war, and so forth. The second skit was based on the question of "What if Superman had been German?" and featured the storyline of young Clark Kent landing not on some Iowa farm, but on some German farmland and was ultimately induced to serve the Third Reich. This story, even as a young boy, provoke din me a question about who we were as Americans. In the college classroom, this story evokes similar responses among my college kids. "It's as if these stories are all tailored to our

American ethnocentrism," they say. "Ya' think?" I reply and smile. The point is that the speculation opens up a whole new line of inquiry and can provide students with unique connections in their brain that will foster better retention of the real story (if there is such a thing.)

The Danger

By thinking "outside of the box" and fostering students' thinking in such a way to make the material relevant to them and their world is dangerous. It may incite revolution. It may incite social change. It may lead to a world where we see the complexities of life, appreciate all of our differences while embracing our similarities and, in the end, make us a better people.

It's ok that we are all still hell bent on "survival." That's kind of what humans do. What we need to recognize, perhaps, is that the age old ways of surviving may not be necessarily the best way to do it today. We may have already crossed the threshold such that the "dog eat dog" strategy is no longer helpful, but hurtful. If that's the case then maybe we ought find alternative ways to insure the survival of humans whereby we maximize the potential of ALL peoples. So, learning from our past will be essential and then making connections and applying those lessons in concrete ways will be critical.

This does not mean abandoning our pasts, our history and forging some fake story about where we have been. Instead, it might simply mean that we re-think and re-envision our cultural heroes. Thomas Jefferson, for example, was regarded as a great American hero. For a brief period among some, he dropped in their esteem because he was a slave-owner who had a romantic relationship with one of his slave women, Sally Hemings. But rather than idolize him or vilify him, perhaps we can see him as a human overwhelmed with contradictions (like we all are) such that he was devoted to liberty and flooded with passion, but was also too weak to publicly confront the hypocrisy. He was, in short, human. Theologian and historian Elizabeth A. Johnson does just such a thing when she re-thinks the life of the Virgin Mary in her work,

Dangerous Memories. Johnson re-interprets Mary's historical life and Biblical life and, in doing so, come to "appreciate Mary's significance for our life of faith and its practice." To do, Johnson suggests, requires us to think about "retrieving her memory in a concrete way." It means that we create a living memory of Jesus' mother such that it serves the people of the Church in a meaningful and actively substantive way. If done right, Mary no longer serves as an abstract, dehumanized icon but a living reminder of humanity and possibility. We can be (and often are at the personal level) motivated by the memories of the dead. Thoughts of my mother might motivate me to complete this manuscript. Thoughts of me in the future might motivate my daughters, friends, or students to accomplish something remarkable too. The connection between the living and the dead comes through the act of remembering. By remembering the past, by remembering the dead, by remembering who we were and where we came from can empower us to find that solution for our long-term survival.

So, history and our memories of the past are not simply vague abstractions in the back of our heads or in dusty old books. They are the keys to our survival. Those memories and those histories, however, have to be actively engaged in and with the dream process so that we can make connections, apply it, and make it a reality. It is only through the dream process that the lessons of our historical past and our memories that we can change the future. It is, as Elizabeth Johnson says, "memory with the seed of the future in it." It is all very dangerous because the process interrupts the present, that swirling-chaos we find ourselves caught in on a daily basis, and forces us to reflect upon what it is all about and what more is possible in the infinity of options before us.

Conclusion

For the past "how many ever" years (maybe 30 years), I have examined the history of our planet's people and more specifically the people of the United States. I have published articles, book chapters, local documentaries and three books. I am a historian who teaches, engages in community service, and publishes—all as part of my obligation to the profession and academia in general. During that time, as I prefaced pages ago, I have always seen the world through the lens of history. I consistently argued that the best way to understand who we are as a people was to understand where we came from, how we got to this point. In short, I argued that history was the best way to understand who we are.

Now, as death seems to be closing in on me pretty fast, I understand that I was completely wrong. There is no way of understanding my state today. You cannot look back at my past and definitively account for the cancer that has invaded me, is slowly killing me, and will soon lay me six feet underground. There is no history. For some cancer patients, the same cannot be said. Smoking as a historical action contributes to millions of deaths. But, my cancer is different. It has no known cause. It does not run in my family and so genetics does not appear to play a prominent role. I did not suffer any major trauma to the leg to induce it (although I did run into a table in my classroom several times). In short, there appears to be no logical historical cause and effect to account for this cancer. It came without warning and it struck its lethal blow.

So, after long reflection and having written what I have already written here, maybe there is some other explanation for who we are. History, as I have noted, is nothing but memory. Memory is simply thoughts that have persisted over time. Dreams are thoughts beyond our control, but shaped by memories. If thoughts are all we are, then my thoughts are dying. Although I have always maintained an optimistic attitude over the course of my life, somewhere down deep the thought of perishing and dying rested in me. And, perhaps, it was that very fear of death that compelled me to become a historian, to remember as much as possible and with the hope that someone would remember me when it is all said and done. So, I have lived a fraudulent life. I lived to remember and to be remembered and, in doing so, maybe didn't live at all. I was trapped in my own worldview and when that world stopped revolving, I was left with a cancer growing exponentially within me.

I had heard the mantra a million times—"Life is too short." For me, it's the truth. It has been. I am blessed, however, in that in the last quarter of my existence, I began focusing on more than simply history and certainly more than myself. I understood that my place on this planet was not to "get" more but to "give" more. I came to understand that I needed to give of my talents and energy and limited wealth and to give back to those who needed it—not just my students, but the poor, the homeless, victims of trauma and tragedy, those marginalized by society, and those crushed by the demands of our modern society.

Existentialist philosopher Jean-Paul Sartre referred to this as "facticity." "Facticity" includes things that are within that "concrete past" or "set in stone" but that have continued to exercise great influence over us because of the ways we have chosen to interpret and remember them. The past is what one is and to ignore that fact is perilous. To deny one's history is to deny one's identity. To disregard one's facticity, this concrete

past, and the continual process by which we are always being

re-made also makes one inauthentic. To ignore the present is

also dangerous, he'd argue. "To forget, or to be forgotten,"

Michael Malone wrote, "is its own kind of death." So, I live in

and for the present with an understanding of that past. And, I

do so not for accumulation but for appreciation, gratitude, and

gifting. Don't get me wrong, I have been honored by the many

awards bestowed upon me, but I believe I was honored because

I was seen as someone who cared. I was seen as someone who

tried to do right, to do well, and make it a better place.

Therefore, in what days remain, I will give.

And so, it all comes to a close. I have been blessed to

live the life I loved. I have been fortunate and privileged that I

was born in a place and at a time and to a family that could

afford me the luxury of these thoughts. Not everyone is so

fortunate. There are children today starving in Appalachia, in

Malaysia, and across East Africa. There are marginalized

peoples pushed to acts of desperation (and terrorism) by to

their powerlessness and poverty. They are in Iraq and

Afghanistan, Oklahoma and Alabama, Indonesia and Sri Lanka.

The world abounds with desperate people. If there has ever

been a time to re-think who we are for the sake of perpetuating

who we want to be, then this may be the time. While I have

been fortunate, I have also suffered along the way. What has

befallen me over the last 50 years has bred within me an

empathy for those desperate peoples. And so while I die from

this horrible cancer, I also know that there are so many more

who are suffering worse, who haven't health care, or a clean

home with running water and electricity. The fact that they die

desperate and hungry buoys me. For how can I complain about

my life, or regret what I have not done, when I have been so

blessed and that what is ultimately going to happen to me will

eventually occur to everyone else. In death, we see our

ultimate humanity. In death, we see the connections between

ourselves and every other individual on this planet, regardless

of race, creed, religion, color, sexual orientation, or ethnicity.

We will all fold back into the chemical fabric of the universe and some of us will be forgotten and some of us will be remembered. Some of us may only live in the vague dreams of those who stayed behind.

BIBLIOGRAPHY

History

Archer, Peter. *The Quotable Intellectual*. Ann Arbor, MI: Adams

Media, 2010.

Aslan, Reza. *Zealot: The Life and Times of Jesus of Nazareth*.

New York: Random House, 2013.

Balasingham, Adele. *The Will to Freedom – An Inside View of*

Tamil Resistance. NY: Fairmax Publishing Ltd,

2003.

Becker, Carl. "Everyman His Own Historian," *American*

Historical Review 37 (2) 1932: 221-236.

Bercaw, Nancy, ed. *Gender and the Southern Body Politic*.

Jackson: University Press of Mississippi, 2000.

Chesneaux, V. *Pasts and Futures or What is History For?*

London: Thames and Hudson, 1978.

Dowd Hall, Jacqueline. "'You Must Remember This':

Autobiography as Social Critique," in Nancy Bercaw,

>ed. *Gender and the Southern Body Politic*. Jackson:

>University Press of Mississippi, 2000: 1-28.

Gergen, K. "Social Psychology as History," *Journal of Personality

>and Social Psychology* 26 (1973): 309-

>320.

Johnson, Elizabeth A. *Dangerous Memories.* New York:

>Continuum International Publishing Group,

>2003.

Kahin, George McTurnan & Lewis, John Wilson. *The United

>States in Vietnam*. New York: Dial Press,

>1969.

Kahin, George McT. *Intervention: How America Became Involved

>in Vietnam*. New York: Knopf, 1986.

Kaufman, Scott Eric. "What tradition does the Confederate flag

>represent? Is it slavery, rape, genocide,

>treason, or all of the above?" *Salon*, 9 July 2015.

Lanzoni, Susan. "Diagnosing Modernity: Mania and Authenticity in the Existential Genre,"

Configurations Winter 2004, v12, n1: 107-131.

Megill, Allan. *Historical Knowledge, Historical Error: A*

Contemporary Guide to Practice. Chicago:

University of Chicago Press, 2007.

Novick, Peter. *That Noble Dream: The "Objectivity Question"*

and the American Historical Profession.

Cambridge: Cambridge University Press, 1988.

Prunier, Gérard . *The Rwanda Crisis, 1959–1994: History of a*

Genocide. London: C. Hurst & Co.

Publishers, 1998.

----------------------. *The Rwanda Crisis: History of a Genocide*

Kampala: Fountain Publishers Limited, 1999.

Ricoeur, Paul. *History and Truth.* Trans. Charles A. Kelbley.

Evanston, IL: Northwestern University Press,

1965.

Rosenzweig, Roy and Thelen, David. *The Presence of the Past:*

Popular Uses of History in American Life.

New York: Columbia University Press, 1998.

Sayegh, Sharlene and Eric Altice. *History and Theory.* New York:

Pearson Education, Inc., 2014.

Zerubavel, Eviator. *Time Maps: Collective Memory and the*

Social Shape of the Past. Chicago: University

of Chicago Press, 2003.

Memory and the Brain

Adler, Alfred. *What Life Could Mean to You.* Center City, MN:

Hazelton Foundation, 1998.

Akhavan, Payam. "The International Criminal Tribunal for

Rwanda: The Politics and Pragmatics of

Punishment". *American Journal of International Law* 90

(3) 1996: 501–510. JSTOR 2204076

Ansbacher, H. and Ansbacher, R., eds. *The Individual Psychology*

of Alfred Adler. New York: Basic Books,

1956.

Arbib, Michael A. and Kilmer, William L., and Spinelli, D. Nico,

"Neural Models and Memory," in Mark R.

Rosenzweig and Edward L. Bennett, eds. *Neural*

Mechanisms of Learning and Memory. Cambridge:

M.I.T. Press, 1976: 109-132.

Austin, James H. *Selfless Insight: Zen and the Meditative*

Transformations of Consciousness. Cambridge,

MA: M.I. T. Press, 2009.

Bartlett, F. C. *Remembering: A Study in Experimental and Social*

Psychology. Cambridge: Cambridge

University Press, 1932.

Bercaw, Nancy. *Gender and the Southern Body Politic.* Jackson:

University Press of Mississippi, 2000.

Bergson, Henri. *Matter and Memory.* Trans. Nancy Margaret

Paul and W. Scott Palmer. London: George

Allen and Unwin, 1911.

Bloom, Howard. *Global Brain: The Evolution of Mass Mind from*

the Big Bang to the 21st Century. New

York: John Wiley and Sons, Inc., 2000.

Bodnar, John. *Remaking America: Public Memory,*

Commemoration, and Patriotism in the Twentieth

Century. Princeton: Princeton University Press, 1992.

Buzan, Tony. *Use Your Perfect Memory.* E.P. Dutton, 1984.

Byrnes, James P. *Minds, Brains, and Learning: Understanding*

the Psychological and Educational

Relevance of Neuroscientific Research. New York: The

Guilford Press, 2001.

Carlson, Neil R. *Foundations of Physiological Psychology.*

Boston: Allyn and Bacon, 1988.

Churchland, Patricia Smith. *Neurophilosophy: Toward a Unified*

Science of the Mind Brain. Cambridge,

MA: M.I. T. Press, 1986.

Cobb, James C. "Divided by a Common Past: History and

Identity in the Contemporary South". *Away*

Down South: A History of Southern Identity. New York:

Oxford University Press, 2005: 290–301.

Dallaire, Roméo. *Shake Hands with the Devil: The Failure of*

Humanity in Rwanda. London: Arrow Books,

2005.

Doidge, Norman. *The Brain That Changes Itself: Stories of Personal Triumph from the Frontiers of Brain Science.* New York: Penguin Books, 2007.

Dowd Hall, Jacqueline. "'You Must Remember This': Autobiography as Social Critique," in Bercaw, *Gender and the Southern Body Politic*: 1-28.

Fentress, James and Wickham, Chris. *Social Memory.* London: Blackwell, 1992.

Gadamer, Hans-George. *Truth and Method.* New York: Continuum International, 1989.

Gaffigan, Jim. *Dad is Fat.* New York: Crown Archetype, 2013.

Gamage, S. and Watson, I.B. *Conflict and Community in Contemporary Sri Lanka.* New Delhi: Sage, 1999.

Gay, Peter. *Freud: A Life for Our Time.* New York: W. W. Norton and Co., 1988.

Gazzaniga, Michael S. "The Biology of Memory," in Mark R. Rosenzweig and Edward L. Bennett, eds. Neural Mechanisms of Learning and Memory.

Cambridge: M.I.T. Press, 1976: 57-66.

Halbwachs, Maurice. *The Collective Memory*. Trans. Francis J.

Ditter, Jr. and Vita Yazdi Ditter. New

York: Harper and Row, 1980.

Hebb, D. O. *The Organization of Behavior*. New York: John

Wiley and Sons, 1949.

Higbee, Kenneth L. *Your Memory*. Marlowe and Co., 2001.

Hofstadter, Douglas. *I Am A Strange Loop*. New York: Basic

Books, 2007.

Howe, Michael J. A. *Introduction to Human Memory: A*

Psychological Approach. New York: Harper and

Row, 1970.

Hutton, Patrick H. *History as an Art of Memory*. Hanover, N.H.:

University Press of New England, 1993.

Huyssen, Andreas. *Twilight+Memories: Marking Time in a*

Culture of Amnesia. Routledge, 2012.

----------------------. "Monument and Memory in a Postmodern

Age," in James E. Young, *The Art of*

Memory: Holocaust Memorials in History. Munich,

1994.

Ingvar, D. H. "'Hyperfrontal' Distribution of the Cerebral Gray

Matter Flowing in Resting Wakefulness:

On the Functional Anatomy of the Conscious State,"

Acta Neurologica Scandinavica 60(1979):12-15.

Irwin-Zarecka, Iwona. *Frames of Remembrance: The Dynamics*

of Collective Memory. New Brunswick,

N.J.: Transaction Publishers, 2007.

James, Paul. "Despite the Terrors of Typologies: The Importance

of Understanding Categories of

Difference and Identity". *Interventions: International*

Journal of Postcolonial Studies. vol. 17 (no. 2) 2015:

174–195.

Kaluza, Maciej, "Memory as a Challenge to Human Existence," in

Anna-Teresa Tymieniecka, ed. *Memory*

in the Ontopoiesis of Life. New York: Springer, 2009:

147-153.

Kandel, Eric R. *In Search of Memory: The Emergence of a New*

Science of Mind. New York: W. W. Norton

and Co., 2006.

Kansteiner, Wulf. "Finding Meaning in Memory: A

Methodological Critique of Collective Memory

Studies," *History and Theory* 41 (May 2002): 179-197.

Kosslyn, Stephen M. and Oliver Koenig. *Wet Mind: The New*

Cognitive Neuroscience. New York: The

Free Press, 1992.

Lanzoni, Susan. "Diagnosing Modernity: Mania and Authenticity

in the Existential Genre,"

Configurations v12, n1, Winter 2004: 107-131.

Lipton, Bruce. *The Biology of Belief: Unleashing the Power of*

Consciousness, Matter, and Miracles.

Carlsbad, CA: Hay House, Inc., 2005.

Luria, Aleksandr Romanovic. *The Mind of a Mnemonist.*

Cambridge: Harvard University Press, 1968.

Malone, Michael S. *The Guardian of All Things: The Epic Story of*

Human Memory. New York: St.

Martin's Press, 2012.

Massey, Irving. *The Neural Imagination: Aesthetic and*

Neuroscientific Approaches to the Arts. Austin:

University of Texas Press, 2009.

McGaugh, James and Norman Weinberger and Gary Lynch.

Brain Organization and Memory: Cells,

Systems, and Circuits. New York: Oxford University

Press, 1990.

Melvern, Linda. *Conspiracy to Murder: The Rwandan Genocide.*

London and New York, NY: Verso, 2004.

Muller, Jan-Werner Muller. *Memory and Power in Post-War*

Europe: Studies in the Presence of the Past.

Cambridge: Cambridge University Press, 2002.

Narayan Swamy, M. R. *Tigers of Lanka: from Boys to Guerrillas.*

Konark Publishers, 2002.

Olick, Jeffrey K.; Vinitzky-Seroussi, Vered; and Levy, Daniel. *The*

Collective Memory Reader. Oxford:

Oxford University Press, 2011.

Olickal, Jeffrey and Robbins, Joyce. "Social Memory Studies:

From 'Collecting Memory' to the Historical

Sociology of Mnemonic Practices," *American Review of*

Sociology 24 (1998): 105-140.

Paschalidis, Gregory. "Towards Cultural Hypermnesia: Cultural

Memory in the Age of Digital Heritage,"

in M. Tsipopolou, ed. *Digital Heritage in the New*

Knowledge Environment: Shared Spaces and Open Paths

to Cultural Content. Athens: Hellenic Ministry of

Culture): 179-181.

Pinker, Steven. *The Blank Slate: The Modern Denial of Human*

Nature. New York: Penguin Books, 2002.

Ramachandran, V. S. and Sandra Blakeslee. *Phantoms in the*

Brain: Probing the Mysteries of the Human

Mind. New York: Harper Perennial, 1998.

Ribot, T. *Diseases of Memory: An Essay in the Positive*

Psychology. London: Kegan Paul French and Co.,

1882.

Rose, Steven P. R.; Hambley, John; and Haywood, Jeff,

"Neurochemical Approaches to Developmental

Plasticity and Learning," in Mark R. Rosenzweig and

Edward L. Bennett, eds. *Neural Mechanisms of Learning*

and Memory. Cambridge: M.I.T. Press, 1976: 293-310.

Rosenfield, Israel. *The Invention of Memory: A New View of the*

Brain. New York: Basic Books, Inc.,

1988.

Rosenzweig, Mark R. and Bennett, Edward L., eds. *Neural*

Mechanisms of Learning and Memory.

Cambridge: M.I.T. Press, 1976.

Roth, Michael S. *The Ironist's Cage: Memory, Trauma, and the*

Construction of History. New York, 1995.

Rutledge, L. T. "Synaptogenesis: Effects of Synaptic Use," in

Mark R. Rosenzweig and Edward L. Bennett,

eds. *Neural Mechanisms of Learning and Memory.*

Cambridge: M.I.T. Press, 1976: 329-339.

Scharer, Martin, "Things+Ideas+Musealization=Heritage: A

Museological Approach," Keynote at

Academic Year of the Graduate Program in Museology and Heritage, PPG-PMUS, UNIRIO/MAST, Rio de Janeiro, 17 March 2008.

Scott, Gini Graham. *30 Days to a More Powerful Memory.* AMACOM Div., American Management Association, 2007.

Siegel, Bernie S. *Love, Medicine, and Miracles: Lessons Learned About Self-Healing from a Surgeon's Experience with Exceptional Patients.* New York: Harper, 1986.

Snyder, Timothy. "Memory of Sovereignty and Sovereignty over Memory: Poland, Lithuania, and Ukraine, 1939-1999," in Jan-Werner Muller, *Memory and Power in Post-War Europe: Studies in the Presence of the Past.* Cambridge: Cambridge University Press, 2002.

Squire, Larry R. *Memory and Brain.* New York: Oxford University Press, 1987.

Szpunar, Karl K., et al. "Memories of the Future: New Insights

Into the Adaptive Value of Episodic

Memory," *Frontiers in Behavioral Neuroscience* 7

(2013): 47.

Terdiman, Richard. *Present Past: Modernity and the Memory

Crisis.* Ithaca: Cornell University Press,

1993.

Tulving, E. *Elements of Episodic Memory.* New York: Oxford

University Press, 1983.

Turan, Halil, "Memory and the Myth of Prometheus," in Anna-

Teresa Tymieniecka, ed. *Memory in the Ontopoiesis of

Life*. New York: Springer, 2009: 5-15.

Wan-Chen, Chang, "A Cross-Cultural Perspective on

Musealization: The Museum's Reception by China

and Japan in the second half of the Nineteenth

Century," *Museum and Society* 10 (March 2012): 15-27.

Yates, Frances A. *The Art of Memory*. Chicago: University of

Chicago Press, 1966.

Yerushalmi, Yosef Hayim. *Zakhor: Jewish History and Jewish

Memory.* Seattle: University of Washington

Press, 1982.

Zerubavel, Eviatar. Time Maps: Collective Memory and the

Social Shape of the Past. Chicago: University

of Chicago Press, 2003.

Zerubavel, Yael. *Recovered Roots: Collective Memory and the*

Making of Israeli National Tradition.

Chicago: University of Chicago Press, 1995.

Zull, James E. The Art of Changing the Brain: Enriching the

Practice of Teaching and Exploring the

Biology of Learning. Sterling, VA: Stylus Publishing,

2002.

Dreams

Adler, Alfred, "On the Inrerpretation of Dreams," *International*

Journal of Individual Psychology 2(1936).

Artemidorus, *Oneirocritica: The Interpretation of Dreams.* Trans.

R. White. Torrance, CA: Original Books,

1975.

Blechner, Mark J. "The Analysis and Creation of Dream

Meaning: Interpersonal, Intrapsychic, and

Neurobiological Perspectives," *Contemporary Psychoanalysis* 34 (1998): 181-194.

Bonuzzi, L. "About the Origins of the Scientific Study of Sleep and Dreaming," in G. Lairy and P. Salzarulo, eds. *Experimental Study of Human Sleep.* Amsterdam: Elsevier Scientific, 1975.

Boss, Medard. *The Analysis of Dreams.* New York: Philosophical Library, 1958.

Breecher, Maury M. "The Biology of Dreaming: A Controversy That Won't Go to Sleep," (http:www.columbia.edu/cu/21stc/issue-3.4/breecher) Accessed 24 August 2013.

Burstein, Andrew. "A History of American Dreams," *The Boston Globe*, 28 April 2013.

Dement, William C. *Some Must Watch While Some Must Sleep.* 1972.

Dewdney, Christopher. *Acquainted with the Night: Excursions Through the World After Dark.* New York: Bloomsbury Publishing, 2004.

Domhoff, G. William. *The Scientific Study of Dreams: Neural Networks, Cognitive Development, and Content Analysis.* Washington, D.C.: American Psychological Association, 2003.

Ellis, Havelock. *The World of Dreams.* Boston: Houghton Mifflin, 1911.

Evans, C. and Newman, E. "Dreaming: An Analogy from Computers," *New Scientist* 419 (1964): 577-579.

Fitzgerald, A. *The Essays and Hymns of Synesius and Cyrene.* London: Oxford University Press, 1930.

Freud, Sigmund. *The Interpretation of Dreams.* [*Die Traumdeutung*, 1900], Trans. and ed. James Strachey. New York: Avon Books, 1965.

Garfield, Patricia. *Your Child's Dreams.* New York: Ballantine, 1984.

Gay, Peter. *Freud: A Life for Our Time.* New York: W. W. Norton and Co., 1988.

Hartmann, Ernest. "Dream," *World Book Encyclopedia*, 1978.

Hildebrandt, F. *Der Traume und Seine Verwerthung fur's Leben.*

Leipzig: Reinboth, 1875.

Hobson, Allan. *The Dreaming Brain: How the Brain Creates Both the Sense and the Nonsense of Dreams.* New York: Basic Books, Inc., 1988.

Hobson, J. A. and R. W. MCarley, "The Brain as a Dream State Generator: An Activation-Synthesis Hypothesis of the Dream Process," *American Journal of Psychiatry* 134 (1977): 1335-1348.

Hofstadter, Douglas. *I Am a Strange Loop.* New York: Basic Books, Inc., 2007.

Keller, Helen, "The World I Live in," in R. L. Woods, ed. *The World of Dreams.* New York: Random House, 1947.

Kelsey, Morton. *Dreams: The Dark Speech of the Spirit.* New York: Doubleday, 1968.

Kruger, Steven F. *Dreaming in the Middle Ages.* Cambridge: Cambridge University Press, 1992.

La Berge, S. *Lucid Dreaming.* New York: Ballantine, 1986.

Massey, Irving. *The Neural Imagination: Aesthetic and Neuroscientific Approaches to the Arts.* Austin:

University of Texas Press, 2009.

McCurdy, H. "The History of Dream Theory," *Psychological Review* 53 (1946): 225-233.

McNamara, P. *An Elementary Psychology of Sleep and Dreams.* New York: Praeger, 2004.

--------------------. "Dreams and Memory," *Psychology Today*, 15 December 2013. On-line: http://www.psychologytoday.com/blog/dream-catcher/201312/dreams-and-memory. Accessed 21 April 2014.

McNamara, P. and D. Barrett. *The New Science of Dreaming.* New York: Praeger, 2007.

Nauhert, Rick. "Dreams are Key to Memory," *PsychCentral.* On-line: http://psychcentral.com/news/2010/04/26/dreams-are-key-tomemory/13157.html Accessed 21 April 2014.

NOVA, "What are Dreams?" PBS Documentary.

Payne, Jessica D. and Nadel, Lynn, "Sleep, Dreams, and Memory Consolidation: The Role of Stress

Hormone Cortisol," *Learning and Memory* November 2004, 11 (6): 671-678.

Seafield, Frank. *The Literature and Curiosities of Dreams*. 4th ed. London: Lockwood, 1869.

Smith, Bryan. "Foucault and Binswanger," *Philosophy Today* SPEP Supplement, 2011.

Smith, R. C. *Royal Book of Dreams*. London: Effingham Wilson, Royal Exchange, 1830.

Stahl, W. *Macrobius: Commentary on the Dream of Scipio.* New York: Columbia University Press, 1952.

Stearn, Jess. *The Sleeping Prophet.* New York: Bantam Books, 1967.

Stekel, Wilhelm. *The Interpretation of Dreams.* New York: Grosset and Dunlap, 1962.

Stevens, Anthony. *Private Myths: Dreams and Dreaming.* Cambridge: Harvard University Press, 1997.

Stewart, Charles. "Dreaming and Historical Consciousness," *Historically Speaking*. January 2013: 28-30.

Van de Castle, Robert L. *Our Dreaming Mind: A Sweeping*

Exploration of the Role That Dreams Have

Played in Politics, Art, Religion, and Psychology, from

Ancient Civilizations to the Present Day. New York:

Ballantine Books, 1994.

Westerink, Herman. *A Dark Trace: Sigmund Freud on the Sense*

of Guilt. Leuren University Press, 2009.

NOTE:

I researched and wrote this work in the last 2 ½ years of my life.

I composed it from my couch as I rehabilitated from

chemotherapy and two major lung surgeries. I did it because I

loved the inquiry. I loved the questions it fostered. I loved

being a historian.

When my last prognosis was made, I accepted and embraced it

as well as any person could have. I hope I did it with grace and

dignity.

I have chosen to publish this work through Createspace

Publishing as I have little hope that the manuscript will go

through the review and editorial process in time for me to see

its completion. I have another manuscript out there in that

academic limbo. I know there are a whole host of problems,

but I am beyond capable of repairing them now. So, this is it.

Made in the USA
Middletown, DE
26 April 2020